How to be
Politically Incorrect

Keith Sharp

HABERFIELD EDITIONS
EXETER

Published in the UK by
Haberfield Editions,
3 Barton Villas,
Dawlish,
Devon, EX7 9QJ

© Keith Sharp 1998

ISBN 0 9515570 1 7

Design and production by
Words and Pictures, Shaldon, Devon
Set in Times New Roman and Arial
Printed and bound by Bartlett Printing, Exeter

1

I've got a little list

Think carefully before reading this book, especially if you are a one-legged black lesbian whose rights have been violated by a chair. You won't enjoy it. Nor will wogs, wops, queers, poofters, victims of traumatic but essentially-pleasurable experiences, their counsellors or even the mild Hindoo, whose fly-blown tiffins have probably bent more genders than all the nuclear power stations put together. Far better to spend your money on a dictionary of slang and find out what the world really thinks about you.

We are, of course, about to discuss political correctness, that strange blend of bullshit and moral censure that restricts free speech and distorts the language. There is hardly a loony Left council in the land that does not go in for such nonsense, performing verbal somersaults in the quest for racial, social and sexual equality. If some animals - notably single mothers and members of the prostitutes' commune - turn out to be more equal than others, that is probably what God intended. Somebody, after all, has to benefit from the corrective process.

p.c. is hardly a new phenomenon. Well before Tony Blair abandoned his principles in favour of office, an old Greek named Socrates was charged with corrupting the youth of Athens by filling their heads with un-godlike notions. He had a nasty habit of posing questions such as: "Look! Why are we clinging to outdated ideology when we are supposed to live in a progressive society?" Despite the remarkable freedom of speech in Athens at the time, this was too much for the powers that were. Socrates was handed a bottle of best Bordeaux, liberally laced with anti-freeze, and told to do the gentlemanly thing. As he died, he turned to his friend Crito and said: "Listen, old cock. See if you can

renegotiate the APR on our loan. We're being ripped off."
He thus proved - as Bertrand Russell was to confirm many
years later - that while philosophers may be mathematically
aware they are not always politically correct.

After the Greeks came the Romans who had their own
way of dealing with political upstarts: they simply sent a
legion to put them down. Those, such as the Jews, who
persisted in making trouble, were either fed to the lions or
nailed to a cross for the daws to peck at. But at least the
Romans were impartial. Aristocrats as well as peasants felt
the tip of a legionnaire's spear. Rich men who failed to
contribute to party funds were reminded that power depends
on money. Those unable to distinguish between p.c. and p.i.
were despatched with monotonous regularity. Senators had
a nice line in falling on their own swords when they
discovered too late that the Hansardo Romano had gone to
press carrying possibly indiscreet remarks.

The problem, especially under the cerebrally-challenged
Caligula, was to know what was in and what was out at any
given moment. Lobby briefings tended to be few and far
between and the official line could change without notice.
Fortunately, Caligula himself was removed before he could
either invade the Falklands or be forcibly enrolled as a fee-
paying member of Mencap. As for the delightful Livia, wife
of the Emperor Augustus and mother of his successor,
Tiberius, she was the arbiter of political correctness for half
a century. Anyone who crossed her or was suspected of
harbouring anti-Livian thoughts ("Is he one of us?") was
promptly murdered, usually with poison. A gift of figs,
bearing the seal of the empress, was a signal to run the bath
and prepare to open a vein.

Latin, like most of those who spoke it, eventually became
a dead language, lingering on only in the Church of Rome.
The British, being barbarians, spoke only a crude form of
Anglo-Saxon which led to misunderstandings and delayed
the onset of civilisation. To make life easier, the king took
over religion and appointed himself OiC monasteries. This
worked quite well as one had only to believe what the king

2

believed to be politically correct. A few hysterical women lost their heads but, as some were still burning their underwear, this was regarded as the lesser of two evils.

To believe anything during the PR (post-Reformation) era was indeed an act of faith. One had to know what to discard and what to accept. Poor old Walter Raleigh, who is responsible for all those no-smoking carriages on British trains, ended up in the Tower for believing the wrong thing at the wrong time. (So much for allowing the queen, one Elizabeth, to wipe her feet on his best doublet!) Had he survived the queen's displeasure, he would no doubt have been named Pipe Smoker of the Year and feted by the legal and medical establishments. Even so, he is remembered with affection by generations of shareholders in the tobacco industry.

A few years earlier, a young lad named Christopher Marlowe was creeping with shining morning face to the King's School in Canterbury to learn how to survive in the world of political intrigue. Kit was not only queer but, like Socrates, capable of corrupting the well-bred scions who shared his bed with atheistical ideas. Not to believe in God at a time when the queen's sister was being persecuted for believing in the wrong sort of god was to live dangerously. Not that Kit eschewed danger. A brilliant scholar, he had done the state some service while a rustic actor named Shakespeare was beginning to fret as he strutted upon the stage at Stratford, getting nowhere. Alas, such was the political climate in 1593 that, despite his friends in high places, Kit became a liability and had to be smuggled out of the country. In a deal of which the KGB could have been proud, he made over the copyright of his plays to the yokel from Stratford and went off to Venice to write about the Jews.

Ostensibly, Marlowe was put to death during a pub brawl in Deptford - the sort of activity often engaged in by residents of the docklands. Will, the rustic scribe, suddenly blossomed, showing a remarkable propensity for classical themes. Strangely, he ceased to write long before he made

3

his final exit although he did manage to scribble a few words for his grave, imploring people not to open it. The world has since obliged lest the dreadful secret of Will's duplicity were exposed. Wouldn't it be awful - especially for academic reputations - if all those plays turned out to have been written by a homosexual heathen up to his neck in espionage and not the God-fearing oaf who spent his days having it off with Anne Hathaway? So, in the interests of literature (to say nothing of religious or political correctness), Will's tomb remains a closed book, much to the relief of Stratford-upon-Avon Chamber of Commerce.

There was no compunction about opening the tomb of the noble Lord Byron. This was because he was regarded as not so much politically incorrect (he had backed the workers in Nottinghamshire) as beyond the pale. Anybody who could bed half the women of England while on the run from the bailiffs must surely arouse a degree of resentment. When the tomb was opened, however, the only thing of interest - at least, to one of his biographers - was a certain part of his anatomy (and we're not talking about his club foot, which had fallen off). The part was found to be of impressive dimensions and probably helps to explain his success with women. Even in those days, a title was not everything. Like Marlowe, Byron found political correctness not to his taste and left England in a hurry. He, too, went to Venice where a charming young lady helped to take his mind off his half-sister Augusta and all those boys he had met in Athens. Later, he went back to Greece where, at the ripe old age of 36, he succumbed to the medical profession.

Between Marlowe and the arrival of Miss Germaine Greer on the scene, many a witch had been burned at the stake and many a view corrected under pressure. Both church and state had ways of making you recant although not everybody responded to treatment. The French royal family showed their contempt for public opinion by eating cake as they mounted the scaffold. The Russian intelligentsia played snowballs as they trudged through the steppes to a new life in Siberia. The Irish, short of snow and

4

not sure what a patisserie was, prayed to God and planted potatoes. When the crop failed, they emigrated to America. Those left behind were either shot by the British or allowed to die of hunger. This was an early example of the politically-correct use of the word 'choice'.

And what of the vile wretches transported to America for stealing a loaf of bread or waylaying the Bristol coach? Moll Flanders, the hero of Defoe's novel, found herself there and even prospered for a while. But, after torturing herself with the sort of doubt that never particularly bothered Lord Byron, returned to London and picked up some really bad habits. Moll, who ended her life on the gallows, was not so much a criminal as a girl trying to secure her future. Like so many of her contemporaries, she suffered from emotional stress which caused her not only to steal but accept money from old gentlemen. Eventually, a desperate government tried to improve the moral tone of the nation by emptying the jails and packing nearly everybody off to Australia.

For most of this century, it was politically unwise to remind Australians that the assisted passage scheme for convicted felons continued until shortly before the outbreak of World War I. Many of the Diggers who fought at Gallipoli or died for the Old Country in the trenches at Ypres may well have been seeds of miscreant Poms shipped to Australia by the gillie's wee lass. (They were certainly not indigenous Aussies, most of whom had been shot by settlers in disputes over land and women.) Suddenly, however, white Australians found it terribly chic to be descendants of old lags who had arrived with the First Fleet. To find such a person up the family tree today is not only acceptable but socially desirable, guaranteeing the finder a place at the Governor-General's table. The only cloud on the horizon - apart from the ratbags calling for the removal of the Queen as head of state - is the early, and possibly incorrect, treatment of the aborigines. If only the squatters had killed them all, as they certainly tried to do, the nation could be at ease with itself. But many survived, going walkabout all over the place until settling in tribal homelands around Maralinga where the wichety grubs glowed with an unusual intensity. So, for the moment, at least, Australia remains a multi-ethnic society with immigrant Chinese and a handful of black fellahs still dreaming of billabongs filled with XXXX.

The current spate of political correctness probably began in America where a few liberated women and one or two publishers saw the chance of making a quick buck. This was not the case in the Soviet Union where p.c. had been a way of life, and death, for most of the century. A certain Josef Vissarionovitch Dzhugashvily, an avuncular Georgian with a droopy moustache, was very keen on the idea. Indeed, anybody who did not share his opinion on everything from Dostoyevsky to collective cucumber quotas was invited to step in front of a firing squad. Later, when the compassionate Khrushchev took over, deviants were given a choice: the salt mines or the psychiatrist's chair. A posting to Gorky, where nearly everybody was mad, came to have a certain cachet.

In both Russia and America, the key to political correctness was the willingness to conform. The Americans probably inherited the trait from the law-abiding folk who settled in Salem before the Italians arrived. Like the Russians, nobody was inclined to rock the boat. Not until a Canadian gentleman, a Professor Galbraith, came along and questioned the conventional wisdom did anyone dare to express heretical views. Since then, all sorts of lunatics have jumped on the bandwagon, each vying to outsell the other's brand of absurdity. Some, like a Professor Friedman, have done quite well, managing to impose a mental straightjacket on the economy. Others have been exposed as charlatans and disappeared into the black hole of history.

How, then, does one define what is correct and what is incorrect? According to the dictionary, correct is "true, accurate, right, proper". Now, you can see at once that 50 per cent of that definition - right, proper - is purely subjective. What is right and proper for the citizens of Salt

Lake City - where not to conform can seriously damage your wealth - may not be quite the thing for ex-swingers in London. In the hands of a skilled lawyer - and in the United States there are more lawyers than people - even what is true and accurate can be turned on its head. Is it true, for instance, that the only way to stamp out the drugs trade is by providing Colombian peasants with an alternative income? The Saudis might argue that their method - death to pedlars - is far more cost-effective. Is it right to stop silly girls having abortions? A lot of respectable, middle-aged matrons who have never felt the surge of passion on a moonlit night would appear to think so. Is it proper, i.e., consistent with the views of the majority, to smoke in public? The people of San Francisco, where such behaviour is banned, think not.

The problem is not to define what is right and proper - anyone with a shred of moral fibre can do that - but to prevent such definitions falling into the hands of a vocal and dedicated minority. Once the spin doctors get to work, even the most innocent words can acquire a different meaning. Most people want to do what is right and proper - that is, just and equitable - without any help from the p.c. lobby. They do not need to be told how to think; in fact, they would prefer not to think. (Just look at the ratings for Eastenders or Coronation Street!) They are quite happy to tag along with the crowd, swallowing all sorts of sanctimonious claptrap, provided it helps them to have a nice day or avoid the charge of being racist, sexist, bloody-minded or simply old-fashioned. If they can recycle the linguistic garbage to their own advantage, so much the better. Thus chairs are placed in control of committees, companies are downsized and human resources optimised to support the prevailing corporate philosophy (of greed and excess profits).

The proponents of political correctness have had things pretty much their own way in recent years and have become the intellectual despots of the age. It is time to call their bluff.

2

Joe's legacy

Are you now, or have you ever been, a member of the Conservative Party? Take care before you reply. Your career may depend on it. To answer 'Yes' could brand you as a relative of the dinosaur, soon to be extinct. In the capitals of Europe, your sincerity and commitment will be open to question. You will be accused of allowing dogma, as well as pride, to dictate your views on everything from a single currency to the size of Lady Thatcher's handbag. At the very least, you will be seen as an outmoded example of the robber baron - an inverse Robin Hood who takes from the poor and gives to the rich.

But it's a foregone conclusion that most of you will not answer 'Yes'. Not because you have never voted Conservative but because you have never joined up. It's the same with all political parties. The vocal minority sets the agenda, the apathetic majority accepts whatever ludicrous theory is the flavour of the month. Herr Schicklgruber, alias Adolf Hitler, had it down to a fine art. He raved and ranted, saying nasty things about Jews, gypsies, communists and anybody else who hadn't employed him to paint their house. The whole nation was enthralled. Even members of the British aristocracy were quite taken with this quaint little madman who could apparently convince people he was quite sane. Whatever Herr Hitler said, particularly to the Gestapo, was not only politically correct but de rigueur. Those rash enough to point out the flaws in his argument were sent to camp where they could concentrate on their own fallibility. Dr Goebbels, the poison dwarf in charge of propaganda, was even able to convince people that concentration camps did not exist. Only when British troops stumbled upon the starving survivors at war's end did the world realise that truth and accuracy were not Dr

Goebbels' forte. And yet, despite the evidence, there were some - including members of the British aristocracy - who insisted that the camps were a figment of the imagination. Mr and Mrs Cohen had simply gone away for the weekend, presumably to discuss the iron curtain which Dr Goebbels thought might shortly descend on Europe.

While Herr Schicklgruber had few close friends, he was not short of allies, most of them nasty bits of work like himself. In Russia, the avuncular Georgian was quietly putting down millions of erstwhile comrades who did not subscribe to his brand of political correctness. Just as upper-class Brits failed to notice any concentration camps in Germany, so members of the Labour Party (that is, the old, unreconstructed and socialist Labour Party) saw few signs of dissent in the Soviet Union. What a marvellous country it was that could take a serf and turn him into a nuclear physicist! Some intellectuals found Uncle Joe's methods of educating the masses somewhat too radical and took themselves off to Mexico where they unaccountably had ice picks stuck in their brains. (It is, of course, very hot in Mexico and an ice pick can easily fall from a glass of tequila.)

In Italy, another demented dictator, a former journalist named Mussolini, treated the natives quite well (a tax on bachelors, concessionary fares for pregnant women) but did lasting damage in the colonies. Arabs caught speaking anything but Italian in school were beaten mercilessly until they could conjugate standing on their heads. Some, not familiar with the verb to conjugate, thought it meant something else and gave rise to yet another story of peculiar Arab habits. Il Duce himself ended life the wrong way up, hoisted from a lamp-post by his heels.

Not that foreigners are always to blame for political excesses. Long before Senator Joe McCarthy arrived on the scene, Reds had been found under many a bed in the United States. Many were not so much under the bed as between the sheets, screwing and being screwed by the WASP establishment and every producer in Hollywood. Along came the thought police and hey, presto! the p.i. coupling was hastily abandoned. Those who had apparently spent such an enjoyable time in the embrace of subversive elements of society could remember nothing about it. Red had changed from an aphrodisiac into an amnesiac. A few managed to remember something, especially the state of their bank account. Like Judas, they were prepared for the sake of a crust to name those who were not 100 per cent American boys and girls - or practically everybody in the film industry. Hollywood was purged of subversive elements, including Charlie Chaplin and Gene Kelly, both of whom sought employment in Europe. Two clean-cut Americans were sent after them to make sure that U.S. embassies and military bases did not succumb to their subversive charm.

The crime of those arraigned by the pathetic and now discredited figure of Joe McCarthy was that they had been politically incorrect. That is to say, they did not share his view of motherhood and apple pie at a time when the conventional wisdom dictated that they should. With the benefit of hindsight, it is easy to dismiss the paranoiac probings of the House Un-American Activities Committee as a symptom of the Cold War. But for those on the receiving end, even if they pleaded the Fifth Amendment to avoid incriminating themselves, it was a traumatic experience. Careers were ruined, relationships dashed and the reputation of the United States (such as it was) sullied for years. And for what? Mainly, it is now clear, for the greater glory of Joe McCarthy.

What, precisely, was the crime of those accused of un-American activities (assuming they had not, like Dr Fuchs, been selling nuclear secrets to the real Reds)? Apart from screwing each other, it would appear that they had been undermining the moral fibre of the nation by dreaming socialist dreams. In the United States, dreams - comprising mainly of chromium-plated dollar signs - are the prerogative of Big Business. And, as everybody knows, what is good for business is good for America. What is good for the downtrodden masses depicted by Steinbeck in *The Grapes of Wrath* or Upton Sinclair in *The Jungle* is obviously subversive. Anybody who could write nasty things about the flivver king (Henry Ford) or the meat barons of Chicago was clearly a troublemaker of the first order. Suppose the downtrodden masses actually read those books or saw the films based on them? Who knows what might happen? It was the patriotic duty of the House committee to nip socialism in the bud.

Of course, we are not talking about the upper echelons of American society where dissenting views are treated with wry amusement or, at worst, a visit to Dr Anthony Clare. Perhaps several visits and a chat on the wireless if the patient looked like becoming an embarrassment. But among the blue-collar workers, the Bible bashers and the downtown office girls who dream of finding a rich husband respectability is all. These are the people whose faith in the system was shaken by the Vietnam War. The mere suggestion that Senator McGovern, the Democratic candidate in the 1964 presidential election, had been to a psychiatrist was enough to sink his campaign and end his career. That his political rival, Senator Barry Goldwater, could suggest dropping an H-bomb or two to clear the jungle in Vietnam was regarded as merely the whim of a Right-wing eccentric. Everybody knew that napalm was far more effective.

The Vietnamese, at least the northern variety, were backed by another crowd of inscrutable Orientals, the Chinese. The chinks had been stopped in their tracks a few years earlier in Korea, a small country to the north of Shanghai that used to be part of the Japanese empire. Barry Goldwater's predecessor in the A-bomb stakes, General McArthur, had wanted to drop a small charge here and there to help reduce the pressure on China's food resources. But the president, not then his old military colleague, Dwight D Eisenhower, but a wimpish civilian, Harry S Truman, would not tell him where the fuse was. So the American Army in Vietnam had to deal with the Chinese again, albeit at second hand. This was just as well for, as General McArthur had intimated, there were an awful lot of them - and none believed in planned parenthood.

Fortunately, the father of the nation, Mao Tse-tung, was about to embark on the literary venture of all time, a little red book containing his thoughts. It was not a very big book but sold by the million and was serialised on all the best walls in China. Not to have read at least one chapter branded you as a dangerous, and possibly radical, intellectual. Once the Red Guards were informed, you were in the same position as a Hollywood scriptwriter who had inadvertently cast aspersions on General Motors. The only work for such people was to stand against a wall and test the velocity of the latest Chinese or American rifle. This helped to reduce the population and temporarily abate the need to take over Formosa, a beautiful island that was once part of the Japanese empire.

The Chinese are today something of an anachronism. There are only about 1,200 million of them, accounting for a fifth of the world's population, but they persist in being Communist. Moreover, their empire is expanding and now embraces Hong Kong, a small rock surrounded by a fragrant harbour that was once occupied by the Japanese. The fact that they are Communists has created enormous difficulties for historians at the Academy of Ancient Iron Maidens. According to the chief executive of AAIM, a Ms Thatcher, Communism no longer exists. The Chinese, being a pragmatic as well as extremely polite race, said that if it no longer existed they would have to re-invent it. Besides, they had no wish to see a lady - even the running dog of capitalism - lose face. So they have compromised by privatising the tractor works at Wuhan. (The Japanese, who bow lower and smile more seductively than the Chinese, lost their status as the world's most polite people by failing to seek permission before they attacked Pearl Harbour. Since then, they have been known as little yellow bastards.)

The female of the Thatcher species - unlike the male, which is seldom seen beyond the drinks cabinet - is an interesting phenomenon. The original was described (or, at least, her policies were) by Ted Heath, an ex-Prime Minister, as an aberration. Some 20 or 30 years from now, this will no doubt prove to be the correct political interpretation although by then historians may well have to explain just what the Conservative Party was. In the 1980s, when the Thatchers were touring the Middle East, waving their arms about and helping the Arabs keep tyrants like Saddam Hussein at bay, the now-rusting lady was not perceived as an aberration. Thousands of people, all members of the Conservative Party, gave her a standing ovation whenever she appeared at a party conference. Like the long-dead sheep who cheered Herr Schicklgruber to the echo, they knew what was politically correct and what was not. Socialism was not and Conservatism - especially the free-market variety espoused by the grocer's daughter from Grantham - was. Only Ted Heath sat there and sneered. But as his mother had been a lady's maid and not a member of the landed gentry one couldn't expect anything else.

Ms Thatcher developed political correctness virtually single-handed into an art form that pervaded all levels of government in Britain. Barely a quango or local authority was spared the sometimes unconventional wisdom emanating from Number 10. The one and only criterion for those wishing to pass muster aboard the Thatcher ship of state was 'Is he one of us?' If he or she wasn't, they were promptly thrown overboard. Many found her presence strangely emasculating and were thus unable to do what comes naturally and poke her in the eye. As a result, Britons suffered a particularly enervating and destructive form of p.c. far longer than necessary. If, indeed, it was necessary at all.

The lesson was not lost on the Labour Party which felt that it had somehow been wrong-footed by conviction politics. To show that it was not simply an adjunct of the union movement, it decided (or rather its leader, Tony Blair, decided) to slough off its socialist past and steal La Thatcher's clothes. Unfortunately, Mr Blair had been so

13

busy chattering to the voting classes in London NW that he failed to notice that the nation was in the mood for socialism again. (His deputy, Mr Prescott, could have told him but nobody thought to ask a former merchant seaman.) The question most frequently asked over the dinner tables in Islington - where opinions mattered - was: Are you now, or have you ever been, a socialist? ('A what? Not me, guv. I don't know the meaning of the word.') Despite the denials and suggestions that the S-word has been expunged from the litany of acceptable words and phrases, Mr Blair continues to blush every time the Old Guard blurts it out in public. The politically-correct way to describe current Labour ideology is 'quasi-Christian but without all that evangelical cant'. Except in Brussels, to which he and his wife have been exiled, it is no longer acceptable to mention that Mr Neil Kinnock was once leader of the party. It is perfectly all right to recall the brief reign of Mr John Smith. Mr Smith is, of course, dead and cannot answer back.

The problems faced by Mr Blair in grappling with God are but little local difficulties compared to the daily dialogue with the Devil that engrosses the Russian leader, Boris Yeltsin. Mr Yeltsin sees devils at all hours of the night and day, sometimes coming out of the woodwork, more often out of a bottle. Sometimes he is forced out of the Kremlin and into a sanatorium (or gremlin dacha) in an effort to shake them off. But, like Dracula, the little devils can slip through the slightest breach of security and sink their teeth into his bloodstream. That's why, after a week or so of unremitting terror, he looks so drained and less than perestroika-fied. Under Joe Dzhugashvily, it would have been politically incorrect to venture an opinion on the health of the leader. But such is the grip of glasnost in the Russian Federation that Mr Yeltsin has to fight his devils in public.

His condition is probably no worse than that of the former president of the United States, one Ronald Reagan, who is thought to be suffering from Saunders Disease (but with no hope of recovery). Ronnie once worked in Hollywood, making B-movies, although he could not remember this, or anything else, when he reached the White House. On a visit to South America, he even forgot which country he was in: it might have been Brazil or even Venezuela. He knew it couldn't be Cuba or he would have been arrested on his return. Perhaps it was Lourdes, where miracles can give you such a wonderful feeling of freedom.

South Americans are not, on the whole, in favour of political dissent. The degree to which it is tolerated depends largely on the level of debt. More debt = more freedom to express views not shared by the Army. But as all South American countries are up to their ears in debt the freedom is relative. On the streets of Rio, the freedom of orphans to breathe is often curtailed by thugs masquerading as police. In Colombia, even the president has to look constantly over his shoulder to avoid death in the afternoon. Why anybody should want to kill him when the country's highest court had cleared him of any connection with the drugs trade is hard to fathom. Perhaps he just has a feeling that the judgement was somehow politically correct. In neighbouring Panama (which was, of course, part of Colombia until the Americans built a canal and installed their own troops there), the president was horrified to learn that drugs money had been used to defray his election expenses. But, at least, that could only happen in a democracy. In Paraguay, law-abiding citizens exude political correctness by reading *Die Welt* and consuming large portions of apple strudel. Some are so poverty-stricken that they still wear old-fashioned jackboots.

As for Dr Fidel Castro, the cigar-smoking tyrant who has run Cuba for the past 40 years, even the World Bank has been unable to curb his excesses. Americans have been warned not to go there and recently this advice was extended to citizens of Canada and the United Kingdom. Apparently, the tyrant keeps pigs in a bay overlooking Florida. When the wind is southerly, the State Department begins to worry about the health of illiterate drug pushers on the streets of Miami. The bureaucrats fear that the

Cubans could be planning an invasion to teach them how to read. Cuban exiles, many of whom are named Batista, already knew the island was unhealthy. They would like to see the pig farm demolished and the site restored to its former glory as a brothel and casino complex. Then Cuba would not have to rely on loans from anybody.

To most Europeans, South America remains a far-off land about which they know little. The enduring mystery is why Sir Walter Raleigh brought back a potato instead of filling his boat with coca plants. This would have provided Britain with the biggest dollar-earner in history and saved the Liberal Democrats a lot of agonised debate over the legalisation of cannabis. Perhaps even in those days Sir Walter was just trying to be politically correct.

2 x 2

No Remission

Imagine, for a moment, that you are Home Secretary. Not the sort of secretary who sits at home, crouched over a personal computer, wondering how to keep the kids quiet, but a politician - perhaps a lawyer - who has climbed to the top (well, nearly) of the greasy pole. Somebody with access to House of Lords notepaper has written to you, alleging that the prisons are overcrowded. In the past, this sort of humanitarian bleat - emanating largely from the Howard League for Penal Reform - caused your predecessors many a sleepless night. But you are made of sterner stuff and not likely to be brow-beaten by a limp-wristed lord, however noble his lineage. Law and order is your prerogative and one of the main planks in your party's manifesto. How do you reply without giving offence, appearing to be arrogant or reneging on your party's commitment?

The obvious answer - and one that is politically correct, albeit somewhat arrogant - is to remind the noble lord that you are Home Secretary, not he. If the prisons are overcrowded, that is because a depressingly large number of people do not know the difference between right and wrong. They must be deprived of their liberty until they have learned to mend their ways. Prison, after all, is about rehabilitation, not merely punishment. For that reason, you are determined to build more and more prisons until the Chief Secretary to the Treasury pleads with you to call a halt. But, for the moment, the Chief Secretary has other matters on his plate and it is your duty to protect potential voters from the ravages of crime.

As a politician, you will obviously need to keep in mind that your own future lies partly in the hands of wrongdoers who for some reason are currently not behind bars. Until they can be caught and returned to choky, you will have to tread carefully, balancing the needs of society against your own dangerously-low majority. It will be helpful, and certainly expedient, to emphasise your commitment to a crime-free environment in which old people can walk the streets at night without fear of being mugged. You might even join the 'Specials' and put your truncheon where the vote is. At home, in the privacy of your study, you will contemplate the latest crime figures and despair. How are you going to keep your seat when the buggers continue to nick things?

History is unlikely to be very helpful. In legal circles, history is known as precedent and can be found in dusty old law books on the shelves of public libraries. Some of it is extremely p.i. and not conducive to winning votes, especially among the bed-and-breakfast brigade who rely on the refugee trade. Moreover, many libraries have been closed through lack of funds and, as a Home Secretary with a record as long as your arm, you could hardly ask a judge to lend you a copy. Most judges are feeble-minded wimps who would just as soon fine a rapist half a crown as send him to Devil's Island.

As a way of reducing the population of French jails, Devil's Island (you will remind the noble lord) was undoubtedly a success. Indeed, many examples of effective punishment can be found in those countries not subject to the humanitarian instincts of feeble-minded wimps. Take Russia, for example. The scribbler Dostoyevsky virtually confessed to raping a little girl in the public bathhouse. Yet such was the state of anarchy under the Tsar that the KGB could not provide the evidence. Instead, he was arrested on some trumped-up charge of being politically incorrect and sentenced to death by firing squad. At the last minute, the Tsar discovered he had no ammunition and decided to exile the literary-inclined child molester to Siberia. There, he extirpated his sins by writing a book called Crime and Punishment. As Home Secretary, concerned with the welfare of little girls and the maintenance of law and order, you might do worse than seek precedent in such a book. In all probability, it will strengthen your feeling that political trouble makers, particularly poll tax defaulters, get off too lightly. For them, a prison in Siberia is not good enough; they need electronic tagging and barbed wire to keep them away from honest citizens.

Closer to home, there is the woman Hindley, sentenced to life imprisonment for a youthful escapade on the moors which resulted in the deaths of several small boys. How will you explain to the noble lord that you have no intention of letting the evil bitch go, even though she is completely rehabilitated and has paid her debt to society? On no account should you be seen to pander to public opinion, especially some vindictive old women up North who would like to see the prisoner kept behind bars for the term of her natural life. In the privacy of your study, you might think there was a case for letting her out; after all, she is unlikely to offend again. But to say so would call for a degree of compassion and political back pedalling that would not be in your long-term interest. So, for the time being, you will continue to insist that early release never improved anybody.

And what about those women in America with chains around their ankles? Doesn't the sight of them, marching into the desert to work off their debt to society, give you a thrill? Perhaps, after writing to the noble lord, you should drop a line to the sheriff of Chain Gang County. He could really be on to something. After all, your colleagues who sat round the table at Number Ten in the eighties never had that sort of buzz; most of them were not even aware they had been emasculated. Besides, the sheriff's other idea - of making prisoners pay for their board and lodging - might enable you to stitch up the Chief Secretary. Anything that will help you to build more prisons and reduce overcrowding is worth looking into.

Clearly, the task of providing more accommodation is not an easy one and - you will inform the noble lord - it is your intention to go away on holiday before reaching any decision. Alas, while soaking up the sun, news reaches you that the prison governors, unable to feed the growing number of offenders, have thrown open the gates to let the inmates fend for themselves. Hundreds of prisoners, many of whom have still not paid their community charge or filled in the register of members' interests, have been turned loose into the night. Some have undoubtedly slunk back to Brixton, where many families who have come down in the world eke out a miserable existence in two rooms.

The open-door policy clearly presents you with an enormous dilemma. Would it be politically correct to fly home on the next plane and give the governors a dressing down? Or do you recall the precedent of an enlightened governor on Norfolk Island who let the wretches have a taste of freedom? Whatever you do, you must ensure that none of the mud sticks to you. It may even be necessary, to maintain your squeaky clean image, to sacrifice a best friend, provided that such a person can be found. If all your friends have been sacrificed long ago, a scapegoat - perhaps somebody hoping for remission - can be encouraged to volunteer. He can then be kicked around the media until he admits his faults and pleads for mercy. Be careful not to use excessive violence, though, as this could prove counter-productive. You don't want another letter from the noble lord or, worse still, from Mrs Mary Whitehouse.

Venting your spleen will probably make you feel a lot better although it will do little solve the problem of how to reduce the prison population. Perhaps the answer lies in all those old warships that are no longer required now that the Cold War has receded into precedent. They could be filled with junkies, rapists, murderers, paedophiles and ministers of the Crown caught fiddling their tax returns. After all, did not a previous Home Secretary fill the hulks along the Thames with drunks and debtors before shipping them all off to Australia? Charles Dickens, whose very own father had to pay for board and lodging at the Marshallsea when he was sadly strapped for cash, wrote about them in one of his books. But that was a long time ago and, unlike Mr Micawber, the current breed of poll tax defaulters is unlikely to find a welcome Down Under.

Perhaps, as a lawyer, you could set up a new international penal zone, such as the Bermuda Triangle in which ships disappear without trace. This would be a lot cheaper than trying to rehabilitate old lags and allow you to wipe your hands of the entire problem. Indeed, the move might prove so popular that Myra Hindley could be persuaded to vote for you, provided she were free.

But, you will remind the noble lord, you have no intention of allowing the permissive society to deteriorate further into the remissive society. Under your regime, the law will be upheld and criminals made to sleep six in a bed. Taking up your pen, you will write to the noble lord as follows:

My Lord,

I have your letter. Your comments have been noted.

Yours faithfully,

Home Secretary

3

Ten little nigger boys

To be born black, or even a light shade of brown, is to ensure that you will be pampered and feted by the p.c. lobby. They will encourage you to believe that you are better than the white trash which has inherited the earth and that the only reason you are downtrodden, exploited and abused is because of the colour of your skin. They will even ensure that you have a headstart in the jobs market not - perish the thought! - because you might lack the intellectual clout to become a research chemist but because of the inherent prejudice of white employers. Unless you happen to run into a lout who calls you a black bastard, or simply nigger, you will grow up to believe that 'anything they can do, I can do better'. You will also have an almighty chip on your shoulder that only the harsh realities of life will cure.

The uninhibited championing of ethnic minorities has helped large numbers of native sons to do rather well for themselves. They have become presidents of some two dozen countries in Africa and the Caribbean and those not in jail or under a shadow of some kind are all statesmen of world renown. In the space of a few short years - from the time Dr Livingstone discovered the falls that supplied their water to the rescue of President Clinton from Somali warlords - they have risen by sheer ability to the highest offices in the land.

There was, for instance, Kwame Nkrumah, a poor boy from the Gold Coast who scrimped and saved until he had amassed a fortune as Number One Bwana of the newly-independent Ghana. Only the most prejudiced white man, struggling to pay the mortgage on his salary as a lowly clerk in the Inland Revenue, would suggest that Dr Nkrumah had anything other than a good accountant and perhaps a few shares in a privatised utility. It would be entirely wrong, and racially offensive, to suggest that he was a corrupt dictator who feathered his own nest. People of his ability cannot be expected to spend their lives in the service of the state; they must be given an incentive or the economy will stagnate. The saving grace of all dictators is that the abused and exploited masses would do exactly the same were they ever to get their hands on the levers of power.

One little black fellah who did manage to grab the levers of power was Idi Amin, a former sergeant in the British Army with a taste for blood sports and some old scores to settle. To say that Giddy Idi was a power-crazed lunatic who ought to have been shot by the Governor would, of course, smack of racial prejudice. He must therefore be described as an African statesman blown off course by the winds of change. Or simply as a little boy who somehow lost his way. While on his wayward course, Amin managed to throw out everybody who had any impact on the economy of Uganda. The bodies of those who did not take the hint and book a seat on the first flight to London were found floating in Lake Victoria. Some tribal elders completely lost their heads which were later found by the chef in the stateman's refrigerator. (Editor's note: Jokes about Africans being cannibals are politically incorrect. They only eat human flesh when no other source of protein is available.) Alas, Idi lost his way so completely that he simply wandered off and has not been seen for many a day. Some say he boarded a plane at Entebbe airport, thinking it was going to Saudi Arabia. Only when the cabin staff informed him that the meals were strictly kosher did he realise his mistake.

Amin and Nkrumah are but two of the ten little nigger boys who sat on the wall of African independence and had a great fall. Dr Hastings Banda, who took over Nyasaland when it became Malawi, clung to power for longer than most. He had only to wave his fly whisk in the direction of a newspaper or television station for the editor to disappear. The victims, if they survived, underwent a miraculous cure in political correction. But more often than not they were never seen again. Dr Banda himself lingered on into a ripe old age. But with the onset of Saunders Disease he began to lose his grip and the ungrateful wretches who had enjoyed his patronage took advantage of his frailty. They said he was not so much a statesman, a confidant of the Queen, but a murderous black bastard who had put the knife into hundreds of political opponents. Not personally, of course; Dr Banda had taken the Hippocratic oath and it was his duty to save lives. He certainly saved his own, even though his reputation was looking a bit threadbare when he eventually passed away at the age, some say, of 99. As for all that money in his various back accounts, that had nothing to do with the abuse of power. It was saved during his service as a humble GP in Edinburgh.

Not all black men live in Africa or come to power simply as a result of de-colonisation. Some worked their way up with the help of the local witch doctor in countries that were riddled with corruption even before they were weaned from their mother's milk. One such was the much-respected Dr Duvalier - or Papa Doc, as he was known affectionately in Haiti, where he practised faith healing for almost half a century before democratically standing aside in favour of his son, the equally-respected Baby Doc. Dr Duvalier, an humanitarian who understood the plight of the oppressed and downtrodden, could often be seen (in official photographs) dispensing money to the poor. To do so without a prescription might, in some countries, be interpreted as an attempt to bribe the electorate. But as there had never been an election in Haiti this could not possibly have been the case. Eventually, an election was held but so highly did the Haitians regard the ruling family that the winner - a reverend gentleman, not enamoured of voodoo or the gun-toting goons who surrounded the ex-president - declined to take over. Many thousands of Haitians, fearing a clash between church and state, caught the first raft to America where, at the time of writing, they are still awaiting the correct political solution.

How the Duvaliers and their fellow blacks in the United States arrived in that part of the world is one of those quirks of history that looked like a good idea at the time but would have been better left unwritten. Their ancestors were, it's thought, shipped to the American colonies, both north and south, as well as to the Caribbean, as slaves. They were captured in various parts of Africa, not by intrepid British adventurers intent on winning a Queen's Award for Exports but by wogs - or, as they prefer to be called today, Arabs. The Arab traders of Zanzibar - then a beautiful island off the coast of German East Africa - organised the supply of able-bodied workers for the plantation owners of Mustique and Mississippi. Had they sent slaves only of the male gender the race question would have died a natural death when Mr Wilberforce arrived on the scene. But the Arabs also sent lascivious black women who, after pickin' cotton all day, fell exhausted on to their backs and prey to any passing buck with energy to perpetuate the race. The products of these liaisons not only developed a new style of music, called New Orleans jazz, but created one hell of a problem for sociologists and law-enforcement agencies. They also provided writers like Mark Twain and Erskine Caldwell with plots for stories, ranging from DNA testing to lynchings. Mr Caldwell's stories, in which barely a nigger escapes with his life, are so politically incorrect that sales have now stabilised at about 200 million copies.

The ethnic cleansing of Uganda by Idi Amin also proved to be politically incorrect - for Amin himself, for the thousands of Asians uprooted from their homes and for Mr Enoch Powell, a Conservative Member of Parliament. Brigadier Powell, who had no doubt been reading one of Erskine Caldwell's stories of Southern incompatibility, warned that the influx of black people would not make life in Britain any more tolerable (the country then had a Labour government). Revealing an intimate knowledge of Roman history, he warned that uncontrolled immigration would lead to "rivers of blood, foaming like the Tiber". While his speech was undoubtedly in tune with the prejudices of the time, it was deemed to be politically incorrect. Under Labour, one did not say such things and Mr Powell was banished to Northern Island. For the last few years of his life, he was forced to vent his spleen on the white-skinned foreigners across the Channel. In today's parlance, he would probably be known as Euro-sceptic.

Another Powell, a four-star general in the American army, had a chance to avenge the imported darkies of the ole plantation when he directed the US-inspired punch-up in the Arabian (or possibly Persian) Gulf. General Powell, who is definitely off-white, announced that he was going to kill half a million Iraqis - or almost everybody in Kuwait. In p.c. terms, that was not a very nice thing to say. It might have been better had he offered to strangle Saddam Hussein with his bare hands. But because General Powell is black he got away with it. Indeed, the president congratulated him on his fervour and devotion to duty. So high did General Powell's star rise that he was even considered as a potential candidate for the White House (sic). As negroes account for only 15 per cent of the US population, such a preferment might have smacked of positive discrimination. On the advice of his wife, General Powell has since changed his mind. But, having spent his entire career in the Army, he would, of course, have been ideally suited to run a militaristic economy such as that of the United States.

On the whole, militaristic economies do not get a good Press, even if they are run by whites. The little yellow bastards who organised the war in the Pacific are in a class of their own. Indeed, while negroes are treated with scorn and derision, the Nips are still hated with passion. Why should this be? The Japanese have centuries of civilisation behind them and are industrious and excessively polite. Could it be that, unlike the negro who, in his natural state, is merely savage, they have a sadistic streak that makes Auschwicz look like a Butlin's holiday camp? Could it be because they have yellow skins and slanty eyes? Surely not. Lieutenant Pinkerton was quite taken with his little Yum-Yum and, had circumstances permitted, would undoubtedly have married her. Moreover, the Chinese are yellow and are not short of torturer or two. In Tiger Balm gardens throughout the Far East, (or Near North, if you live in Australia), idle wretches can be seen having their tongues cut out, their bellies split with bamboo canes and being put to death in a myriad of subtle ways. These tableaux enliven many an otherwise dull afternoon and are visited by Chinese in their millions. Yet the Chinese do not arouse the same animosity. Had the Chinese and not the Japanese been the enemy during World War II, British and Australian PoWs might be less keen on spring rolls and more in favour of shushi bars. But a more likely explanation, albeit a politically incorrect one, is that the Japanese are superior. While negroes like to think they are superior, the Japanese really are. This does not go down terribly well with car salesmen in Detroit or bitter ex-prisoners who see them only as under-sized automatons with a penchant for sadism.

One reason why the Japanese are seldom invited to share a joke with members of the Burma Star Association is their inability to say sorry. If only they had apologised for bombing Pearl Harbour or putting prisoners on a meatless diet, they might not have been reduced to pacifism. But saying sorry and admitting you're wrong does not come easily to a people who, over the past 100 years, have taught the British, Russian, Chinese and Americans how to kow-tow. It's also difficult to apologise when the history books - that is, Japanese history books - insist that you've done nothing wrong. In 1996, some 50 years after the Japanese laid down their arms to make love, not war, the Prime Minister did, in fact, acknowledge the existence of some ageing Korean women. These women, when they were young and voluptuous, had been recruited by the Imperial Army to 'comfort' the troops and enable them to make both love *and* war. Now less than voluptuous and worried about their future, they demanded compensation - not charity, or presents, as such gifts are known in the West, but real money from the Japanese Treasury to buy cakes and saki. Mr Hakimoto, bowing ever so slightly, said he would look into the matter. The history books will no doubt be revised in due course.

The former Prime Minister of Singapore, Mr Lee Kuan Yew, knows how hard it is to say sorry. Mr Lee, now retired, ran Singapore for 30 years, transforming it from an old-fashioned, colonial outpost full of Somerset Maugham characters into a dynamic island economy totally devoid of character. Any old-fashioned characters, including a Mr Bernard Levin, who had the temerity to turn up at the airport and disagree with him were given short shrift. Hippies with long hair were also given a short back and sides, courtesy of the state. Some ill-mannered brats had their bottoms smacked. In all things, Mr Lee, a Chinese lawyer, was politically correct. Nobody, except Mr Levin, ever suggested that on some occasions civil liberties might just have been compromised. Mr Lee's political opponents certainly didn't and, even if they did, their views were not worth reporting. Only Mr Levin, a wishy-washy liberal, evaded the censor by writing scurrilous articles about the regime from the safety of a heavily-guarded fortress at Wapping, England. Eventually, somebody was found to say sorry: sorry for trading futures without authority and for spotting the gap in the island's regulatory framework. The fall guy, a Mr Leeson, is now learning to eat with chopsticks in Changi jail along with indigenous troublemakers who should have said sorry but didn't. (Strangely enough, the Bank of England, which cast a paternal eye over Mr Leeson's offshore accounts, is itself very reluctant to say sorry. Motto: never explain, never apologise.) As for Mr Lee, he has never apologised for calling Australians white trash. To have done so might have implied that he had once been politically incorrect.

4

The Wrong Sort of God

The British Army knows how to keep the peace, goddamit! That's why, in the officers' mess, it's not quite the thing to discuss politics or religion. Anything else - the sexual prowess of the giant porcupine, the decline of Page 3, the economic prospects for a world without petrol - is fair game. But were somebody to mention the possibility of women priests in the Church of England or the distribution of pederasts within the Church of Rome they would be drummed out of the regiment. Why? Because half the wars that ever were owe their origin to the superstition known as religious belief.

In the beginning, Man created God because Professor Stephen Hawking had not then developed a plausible theory to explain how we all came to be here. Over the years, God went forth a multiplied, fathering a whole range of lesser deities, each responsible for some aspect of the human condition. Many gods lived in the hills, amusing themselves by writing clauses for insurance companies or sending down messages on tablets of stone. But, as is inevitable in a competitive environment, some fell by the wayside and their followers were either snapped up by the survivors or killed in battle, according to custom. The war in Bosnia, the continuing conflict between Jew and Arab, the weird and wonderful groups that put cyanide on the underground or beat their breasts till the blood flows can all be ascribed to God in one form or another.

In fact, there is not much difference between the Moslem fundamentalists, who keep their women in veils, and the traditional wing of the Church of England, which won't have women at any price. The interminable arguments over the ordination of women, which revealed schisms almost as deep as those within the Conservative Party when not at prayer, seriously damaged the ecclesiastical health of those involved. Poor old George Austen, the archdeacon of Leeds, was voted off the church's governing body, the Synod, because of his implaccable opposition to women in the pulpit. To have placed a few twigs under the Maid of Orleans might have been the best way of dealing with such matters in the 12th Century; in the 20th, it is held to be sexist and politically incorrect.

The question that has to be asked is: who cares? The number of practising Christians in the UK is but a fraction of the population as a whole. Even the Regents Park mosque is run by the Saudis. Most Britons (except those in Northern Ireland) are today what used to be known as little heathens, preferring to obtain their view of heaven from a satellite or space probe. The idea of a Supreme Being among the clouds, advising Michael Fish and sending the occasional thunderbolt to frighten the Bishop of Durham, is not one that retains much credence. As Marlowe, the pagan poofter, observed 400 years ago: "I count religion but a childish toy and hold there is no sin but ignorance."

The trouble is that many people (especially those in Northern Ireland) take their religion rather seriously. To them, it is not a childish toy but a way of life. They will send dollars to anybody who can come up with a better interpretation of the Gospels - but woe betide those who suggest that the Koran is full of Ratnerisms. As the author Salman Rushdie discovered, they have ways of shutting you up.

The world's oldest religion - and one that is refreshingly free of dogma and rigid beliefs - is Hinduism which has a number of gods and millions of followers in India. It would have had more but for an unfortunate incident in 1947 when the country was split in two. The souls of many Hindus became disembodied at the instigation of the Moslems, or Pakistanis as they were later called. The Hindus retaliated by despatching a vast number of Pakis to Paradise. (The man in charge of the country at the time, Lord Louis Mountbatten, a Protestant of royal lineage, was later killed by Catholics in the north of Ireland.) The only way to be really safe in India is to be a cow. To the Hindu, the cow is sacred - so sacred that some 200 million of them wander freely about the country, trampling the crops of Hindu, Moslem and Buddhist alike with commendable impartiality. Will the Hindus cull their cattle? Will they hell! They would rather die than shoot a cow past its milk-by date. In fact, cattle are held in such high regard that Hindu statues are said to creep into cowsheds at night to lap up lactose.

The responsibility for keeping Hindu battalions up to strength rests largely with Shiva, the god of fertility. Shiva is often depicted with an erect penis - a provocative pose at the best of times and downright contemptuous in the politically-correct world of vasectomy. Just to confuse matters (or perhaps bring him into line with trendy clerics in the Church of England) he/she is often represented as half man, half woman. Shiva has no heavenly abode but lives under a tree on Mount Kailash in Tibet, or wherever he can erect his penis without incurring the wrath of the Neighbourhood Watch.

The desire to let all creatures (except, of course, Moslems) end their lives naturally, surrounded by their families, reflects the gentle nature of Hinduism. It's a trait shared by the Jains, the fundamentalists of Buddhism. The Jains tend to be a snooty lot, much given to working with diamonds and the finer things of life but drawing the line at spreading cow dung. They have no god but a number of rules, including one which adjures them not to harm any form of life. The monks wear gauze masks to avoid swallowing any passing inset and refuse to eat after dark lest anything falls into their food and is devoured by mistake. During the day, they sweep the path ahead of them to avoid treading on any living creature. Even the smallest organism is revered, including the bacteria which thrive on all Indian foodstuffs.

Mainstream Buddhists are also a godless bunch, putting their faith in the teachings of several ancients, all renowned for their fat stomachs. The original Buddha, Gautama

Shakyamuni, was for many years ascetically thin. He was born into a princely family in north India some 500 years before Christ and led a very sheltered life. One day, he was taken into the street and shown how the other half lived. The scales, he said, were lifted from his eyes. He saw beggars, the old, the sick and the dying. But, instead of castigating them for being a blot on the landscape, he left the palace to join them. Like Shiva, he spent much time under a tree, meditating, until he saw the light (probably of an approaching yak patrol). Since then, he has been known as the Enlightened One. People came from miles around to discuss the meaning of life but he refused to speculate on the existence of God. He was, he said, only interested in the here and now - short-term expediency to help people improve their lot.

In time, Buddhist philosophy spread far and wide but mainly over the hills to the north. The Chinese, or Unenlightened Ones, had their own ideas about the meaning of life - none of them very conducive to longevity. Their methods of birth control, in particular, were somewhat crude. Both male and female children who were likely to eat more rice than the nation could afford were left on the hillsides to die. Old people were dragged off to the killing fields and, like seals, clubbed to death. Their souls, thus released, sped back to earth and were recycled by the next generation. Over the centuries, the Chinese developed a guilt complex about the enforced release of souls and now revere their ancestors. Their attitude towards children is still somewhat ambivalent.

By coincidence, many of the hillsides used as makeshift cemeteries were in Tibet where the skinhead followers of Shakyamuni had stopped to seek the way. The chief skinhead, the Dalai Lama, was becoming a damned nuisance, banging gongs and calling to his followers on distant peaks at all hours of the night and day. The noise was enough to awaken the dead - which is precisely what the Chinese didn't want. Eventually, they told him to get on his bike and hop it. The remaining skinheads, seeking the meaning of life in the jails of Lhasa, waited patiently for the light to illumine their oppressors.

Far to the west, among the sand dunes of Judaea, there lived another race of wanderers, the Jews. Strangely enough, the uncrowned king of the Jews, one Jesus (or Yus Asaf), is said to be buried not far from the Buddha's birthplace. His tomb can be found at Srinagar in Kashmir, alongside that of Nazir-ud-Din, a follower promoted to saint in the 15th Century. According to legend, Yus Asaf got tired of hanging in a state of suspended animation, un-nailed himself from the cross and made his way to India. There, among the hills, he looked for his Daddy (he was, of course, the son of God) and ministered to the lost tribes of Israel who, presumably, had been given wrong directions on the road to Damascus. Eventually, he died at the ripe old age of 120. Not far away, on the summit of Mount Niltopp, is the tomb of Moses who apparently lost his way in the desert and ended up in Kashmir. His tomb is still tended by an isolated Jewish community on the mountain. Both tombs attract their share of tourists. But, as the former Bishop of Durham, the Right Reverend David Jenkins, once remarked, one shouldn't take these things too literally.

It came to pass that over the years other Jews, fed up with finding unexplained organic matter in their meals after dark, hit the trail and headed for Europe. There, they settled down in shtetls, or ghettos, apart from their neighbours. To distinguish them from the Arabs, who came from the same racial stock, the Jews let their hair grow and learned to read. Except for the stupid ones, who stayed in the ghettos while they were being bombed, the Jews are renowned as an exceptionally clever and gifted people. Too clever by half for the average hard-up European which explains why so many of them were beaten to death.

The Jews have always been the underdog, excluded from polite society and the very best of English public schools. They have been kicked out of Spain, Russia, Poland and even the London Stock Exchange. It is hard to say why they were kicked out: nobody has ever been able to explain whether it was because of their race or religion - or whether the two were one and the same. Perhaps it was just because the neighbours didn't like the wailing and gnashing of teeth that accompanied the evening meal, especially in poor quarters where there was nothing to eat but bagels and gefiltfish. Since 1948, however, the Jews have had their own patch of desert on which to grow oranges and atom bombs. They have done both.

The move, sanctioned by the British government, will probably go down in history as the most politically inept ever made. It has demonstrated just how unpopular the Jews can be, and why. No longer persecuted, they have turned to persecuting others. Arabs have been forced off their land and told to take the next caravan to Kashmir. Jewish settlements have been extended up to the Golan Heights in Syria and across the river into Jordan. In 1967, when the Arabs launched a six-day war, the sympathy of the world was with the Jews. Were they not the plucky little fellows who had withstood the Wehrmacht and blown up the King David Hotel? They were, but times have changed. The rabid rabbis of the West Bank have shown how to lose friends and alienate people. The Jews are back where they started, religiously correct but politically on the wrong side of the mountain.

The mountain looms large in the history of Islam, the youngest of the mainstream religions. The Prophet Mohamed, determined to prove that he was a flexible and pragmatic son of the desert (he was born at Mecca, in Arabia, some 600 years after Yus Asaf was entombed in Kashmir), is said to have visited the mountain when it refused to come to him. Latter-day Moslems are not always so flexible. Islam contains (or tries to) the most fanatical bunch of ayatollahs found anywhere, the fundamentalists. Any suggestion that the fundamentalists, who live mainly in Iran, are simply anti-American is totally untrue. They are anti everything, including the Sunni wing of their own religion. It is sheer coincidence that Saddam Hussein, the much-loved ruler of Iraq, was backed by the Americans during the eight-year war with Iran.

Allah, the all-powerful but nevertheless merciful god of the Moslems, demands obedience. The faithful are called to prayer five times a day, kneeling in the direction of Mecca when the do so. There are no priests but a strict moral code, much admired by Mr Lee in Singapore, that keeps the young on the straight and narrow. Provided, of course, that the young of one sect, the Sunnis, do not take it into their heads to plunder the assets of the other lot, the Shias. To be politically incorrect in the bazaars of Basra is therefore terribly easy and can lead to an early appointment in Samarra, or Paradise, as it is known to the devout.

That Allah is merciful can be seen from the fact that most of the world's major reserves of oil outside the former Soviet Union and the United States are to be found in Moslem countries. The richest man in the world is probably the Sultan of Brunei, whose tiny corner of Borneo reverberates with the prayers of the grateful. On the other hand, Allah has proved to be politically careless in the distribution of manna. He has endowed both the Saudis, who uphold Islamic law down to the last infidel, and Colonel Gaddafi, who regards mosques as extensions of his own power base. The blacks in Africa have been largely ignored.

One of the tenets of Islam, and a laudable one at that, is that the faithful shall help each other, especially when one is rich and the other poor. Some of the poorer brethren allege that the richer Moslems have not done enough for their co-religionists. Nonsense, say the Gulf Arabs, still smarting from an expensive war with Saddam Hussein. Just look at the Bank of Credit and Commerce International. When it collapsed, with debts of £1 billion, it was owned by the Sheikh of Abu Dhabi. Many of the customers lucky enough to get their money back were dark-skinned Moslems from Pakistan and London. It was the Sheikh who picked up the bill.

The riddle of the hydrocarbons beneath the sands is one that constantly exercises the Moslem mind. What will happen when the oil runs out? Will the fundamentalists, eschewing all forms of materialism, have won the day? Or will the princes of petroleum have saved enough money to keep the economy ticking over while the people find something else to do? The one thing they will not do, at least while the oil still flows, is find another faith. Under Islamic law, an ex-Moslem is a dead Moslem. Allah may be merciful but he is not terribly keen on Switch cards.

For the time being, however, Islam continues to attract converts, especially in the United States. Millions of black Americans, tired of the white man's god who takes their money but gives little in return, now pray to Allah. During the annual pilgrimage - the haj - they flock to Mecca to fraternise with their fellow believers from around the world. For a few weeks, the desert airport near Jeddah is busier than Heathrow. Hotels, taxis, booksellers all do a roaring trade - but then Mecca always was a centre of commerce. The Saudi police try to keep order and prevent infidels joining the throng. Every Moslem is pledged to visit Mecca at least once before he dies - or die in the attempt. Many collapse at the airport, overcome with emotion. Some die on the desert roads from heat stroke or exhaustion. Others are trampled to death in the crush around the Kaaba, the holy black stone in the Great Mosque. All are guaranteed a place in Paradise, which probably explains why Islam is once again the world's fastest-growing religion.

From the brotherhood of Islam to the bigotry of Northern Ireland may be a small step for God but is a giant leap backwards for mankind. The primitive Bible-bashers of Ulster are authentic relics of the Dark Age who have neither seen the light nor had the darkness lifted from them by a long-suffering guru. (Gu - darkness; ru - remover.) The Orangemen, as they are called, have only one - very simple - belief; that they have a divine right to carry a British passport. Any suggestion to the contrary causes them to froth at the mouth and demand a politically-correct retraction. If this is not forthcoming, they put on bowler hats and march through Catholic areas, banging drums to frighten the devil (or Pope, as he is known locally). Sometimes the devil gets his own back by encouraging supporters to breed like rabbits while the enemy is singing hymns. Unlike the Buddhists, the Protestants of Northern Ireland have not yet learned to sit quietly under a tree and meditate. Perhaps the accumulation of bile makes the lotus position difficult to sustain.

Clearly, for those wishing to be p.i., even to the extent of being burned at the stake, religion offers the best scope. At almost any time of the night or day, to believe in the wrong sort of god will incur the displeasure of somebody, somewhere. In all probability, the heretics will be numbered not in twos or threes but in millions. If you are lucky, you can find an entire country, such as the former Yugoslavia, where merely by crossing the road it is possible to be socially, religiously and politically incorrect at the same time. When that happens, you can be sure that vast amounts of blood will be spilled in the name of God.

As Lieutenant Forgy of the U.S. Navy observed in Pearl Harbour on December 7, 1941: "Praise the Lord and pass the ammunition."

Bonus 4

Great Balls of Fire!

> Come, and let us cast lots, that we may know
> for whose cause this evil is upon us. So they
> cast lots, and, being a roll-over week
> (estimated jackpot: £23m), the lot fell upon
> Jonah.
>
> Old Testament, plus
> Numbers 6, 19, 24, 31, 38 and 42.

Despite a distinct lack of zeal among the wage slaves of Britannia, opportunities abound, yea, yea, for men with a mission to short-change society. All you need is a charming smile, a numbered bank account and a healthy contempt for human nature. Add one meaningless slogan and - hallelujah! - you're in business.

For those who know the ropes, religion is already quite a nice little earner. For those who don't and have a large portfolio of property investments, mainly green-field sites without planning permission, it can be a bit of a let-down. In America, where religion is a very serious business indeed, the men of God have their own radio and television stations. Sometimes, it's hard to tell the difference between the commercial and the Message. Not that it really matters - so long as the money rolls in. Cash is preferred. In the studios, where the money is counted, the rule is: a dollar for God, and one for the counter. Many preachers are now quite rich, having forgotten their mission to drive needles into the eyes of camels. In Rome, where the authorities are still wondering what happened to the billion dollars placed on deposit at the Banco Ambrosiano, the Pope's advisers stick pins into stock-martket quotations and pray that their luck will change.

Not surprisingly, something seems to be missing from

mainstream beliefs. The Jews, the Christians and the Moslems all worship the same god, albeit by a different name. This has caused a certain amount of confusion, with each sect blaming the other for the wrongs of the world. The Jews, who had first claim to Abraham and jealously guard Jehovah, can do nothing right. The Moslems are split between Sunni and Shia while Christians have to put up with popes, prelates, archbishops on the boards of busted banks and reverend gentlemen in Northern Ireland. Even the Buddhists have little local difficulties to say nothing of the fire worshippers who commit suicide on Swiss mountains or swallow poison in the jungles of South America. Clearly, anybody who can heal the spiritual wounds of the world - even by material means - is going to make a fortune.

In fact, the new god is at hand and half the population already sold on the idea. Mahmoun al Otto (may his tribe increase) just needs to be a little up-dated - perhaps by declaring an additional midweek sabbath - and infinite riches will flow in perpetuity. Mahmoun - or Lotto, as he is known to disciples - already attracts vast amounts of gold, if not frankincense and myrrh. But how is the budding entrepreneur to share these riches? Mohamed, the messenger of God, who travelled the sandy wastes of Arabia long before they revealed the true secret of wealth, may provide a clue. He thought the best way to establish his religion and put it on a sound financial footing was to attack the caravans en route to Damascus. He thus obtained not only gold with which to support his growing tribe but a lot of new followers who preferred to believe in Allah rather than have their heads cut off.

Mohamed had a tremendous advantage over Jews and Christians that could be used to advantage by adherents of Lotto. He received his instructions direct from God, usually while lying down and sweating profusely. He, or one of his mates, wrote them down there and then, while they were still revelations. The baby Jesus, on the other hand, had to make do with Numbers recorded by strangers many years later. While these often proved to be inaccurate or out of date, Mohamed prospered. Within a hundred years, the

Prophet's word had spread far and wide. Islam became the greatest power in the world, enabling it to levy a poll tax on vanquished tribes.

To ensure that the new religion gets off to an equally flying start, it might be an idea to procure a set of instructions, easy to follow and which will prove, if necessary, infallible. Fortunately, a set already exits, cobbled together by the very same people who introduced the poll tax to Britons. Lotto's Creed, as it is known, is best studied by lamplight in the late hours of the Jewish sabbath. It has only one defect: it is completely devoid of moral principles. However, this need not deter anybody who is determined to concentrate on the material, rather than the spiritual, side of life.

Like many gods, Lotto is more than just a figurehead. He is the Supreme Being of the technological age and has already proved his virility by siring offspring in a number of countries. In Spain, for instance, the infanta is known as El Gordo, the Fat One, because of his insatiable appetite. El Gordo's riches are distributed among the faithful every Christmas to the ritual chants of innocent choirboys. (They themselves are not allowed to take part in the full ceremony until they are of age.) Lotto has also attracted followers in countries as far apart as Australia and Argentina.

In some respects, Mahmoun al Otto and his offspring resemble the primitive idols worshipped by the Romans and Arabs. Many of these had small holes in the head (as, indeed, did many of the worshippers) to facilitate the insertion of coins. In China, offerings of paper - and even food - were placed in the mouth of omnipotent deities. (This should not be confused with the Hindu practice of placating their gods by offering them milk.) As the Supreme Being of the technological age, it is only appropriate that Lotto should opt for a hole in the wall - although a hole in the head makes a very profitable combination.

Lest cynics within the established churches suspect your motives in setting up a rival religion, you should have a handy set of values. These can be trotted out at times of moral indignation when Lotto has failed to reward the faithful. They should cover a wide field while avoiding undue emphasis on the unfashionable creed of greed. At the simplest, the rules could proscribe drinking, smoking, gambling, whoring, wife beating and drug peddling. Lying and cheating could perhaps be absolved on payment of a small sum, delivered to the nearest temple of Mahmoun in a plain brown envelope. To avoid alienating the upper classes and Conservative Members of Parliament, Lotto would put sexual relations on a sound, but realistic, moral footing by encouraging polygamy. As leader, you would enjoy unrestricted access to the opposite sex. If challenged, you need only point out that Mohamed had 11 wives when he died, worn out, at the ripe old age of 62. (It would be inadvisable to trumpet the fact that his favourite wife, Aisha, was only nine when he married her. Lotto must not only be tough but seen to be tough on the causes of child abuse.)

Only one hurdle remains; that of finding a virgin territory in which to spread the word. The Western world is virtually full of little Lottos, all clamouring for sustenance among the debris of the old religions. The Chinese have their own god, Mahjong, a distant cousin of Mahmoun. That leaves only Russia which, until very recently, was in the grip of idolators. The Russians are crying out for the spiritual and material guidance that only Lotto (and perhaps one or two Sicilian gentlemen who have already set up their tents) can provide. So starved is this huge land of enterprise that a fortune awaits those who can offer any hope of salvation. It could be you.

5

A touch of Harry in the night

Of all the assaults on the English language in recent years, none has been more pernicious than that perpetrated by the queers and perverts of society. It is now almost impossible to use the word 'gay' - meaning light-hearted and sportive - without a sexual connotation. Appropriately enough, the dictionary also defines gay as 'dissolute, immoral, living by prostitution', which aptly sums up the majority of poofters. There is nothing light-hearted or sportive about the dirty old men who hang around public lavatories or try to infiltrate boys' clubs. They are a menace to society. But to call them sodomites - as the Marquess of Queensberry labelled Oscar Wilde - is not only to display an irrational prejudice but to infringe their civil liberties. It is illegal to deny a poofter a job on the grounds that he might corrupt the workforce. Even to think in such terms is, of course, politically incorrect.

There have always been queers in the world and there always will be. Nature will see to that. The latest theory is that a rogue gene, perhaps inherited from Mummy, might be responsible. If so, it is possible that one day regular, i.e., normal, couples (not the sort who get married in Denmark) will be able to determine whether the embryo he in Mummy's womb might prefer to be a she. In which case, they might well opt for an abortion to save the English language from a further bashing by queers. On the other hand, there could be some regular couples with warped minds who want only a child flawed in its genetic make-up. A perfectly healthy foetus that in the normal course of events might grow up to be an Adolf or an Idi could, after proving hetero positive, be quietly aborted.

The number of homosexuals in the community is difficult to quantify. Some estimates put the figure as high as ten per cent of the male population. If so, one gay old dog on a crowded commuter train need only wander into the next carriage to have a choice of partners. This almost surely suggests - no doubt to the relief of fellow travellers - that the figure is far too high and could easily be decimated. Even so, that one per cent of poofters today exerts an influence far out of proportion to its actual size. Queers can be seen coming out all over the place, demanding equal rights and an end to discrimination. Some even try to adopt children. Yet, apart from a few intolerant yokels, few people actually dislike homosexuals. After all, Ivor Novello was one, Somerset Maugham was one, Noel Coward was one. All were talented individuals who gave immense pleasure to the genetically orthodox public.

The trouble with the new generation of queers is that they have not yet learned how to behave like gentlemen. The grubby little oiks who perform intimate services, often to pay the rent, have allowed the freedom from prosecution to go to their heads. As Mrs Patrick Campbell said: "I don't mind what you do so long as you don't do it in the street and frighten the horses." The gay Lotharios who persist in coming out not only do it in the street but flaunt their perversions from every doorway. It is hardly surprising that they have contrived to alienate the overwhelmingly heterosexual public.

In the good old days, when homosexual acts (even between consenting adults in the back of a vintage motor car, somewhere in Hampshire) was a crime, poofters could be blackmailed - and often were by those who knew their little secret. Very often, the blackmailers were those who had taken part in the illegal act. Angus Wilson, the writer, was frequently visited by young men in need of money. Oscar Wilde went to jail after being morally blackmailed by the entire nation. Ivor Novello, jailed for using illicit petrol during the war, is thought to have received a stiffer sentence than the offence warranted because the judge disliked homosexuals. In the liberated climate of today, the victim of homosexual assault will be tested for Aids, offered counselling - and might even receive a visit from the chief constable of Manchester.

Should we feel sorry for somebody born with a defective gene that leads him or her to prefer the same sex? Not if they are getting as much pleasure out of the experience as many of them clearly do. The entire culture of the Middle East is based on the fact that men hold hands and kiss each other in public. Lawrence of Arabia, an unmarried Englishman who spent much of his life on camels, saw nothing wrong with that. The Arabs, after all, prefer little boys, regarding women as the bearers of children. The problems for western societies arise when lots of genetically bent little boys are let loose to ply their sordid trade without legal, moral or sexual restraint. Like stallions turned out to grass after a long winter in the stables, they exhibit all sorts of unnatural behaviour.

The Army (of which Lawrence was a member) has lately woken up to the fact that not all the lads and lassies who signed up to fight for their country have a sufficient blood lust. They have lust all right but not for the enemy. Some of them quite like the sergeant-major, bristling with manhood as he struts about the parade ground with his swagger stick. Why the top brass should only just have tumbled that some men absolutely adore being bullied is hard to fathom. Did not military intelligence suspect that one or two of the nice young men forced into uniform during National Service might prefer to wear something more frilly at night? Did not the camp commandant notice how oddly some of them marched? Perhaps they did but in those days the War Office (and the Admiralty) was staffed by Russian spies with bent genders. To suggest that our own forces were a lot to be desired might have undermined morale and prolonged the Cold War.

The gist of the Army's case in its efforts to weed out homosexuals is precisely that: that they are bad for morale and efficiency. Suppose, for instance, that the adjutant took a fancy to the corporal in charge of the company's database. The affair would be a military and social disaster. The corporal - computer expert or not - would not be able to concentrate knowing that he could never be invited to dine in the officers' mess. And, even in mufti, the captain might well think twice before venturing into the Naafi. The Army is about rank as well as discipline. And suppose that a pair of equally-matched queers - two pips each - were assigned married quarters. Good heavens! The baby-sitting roster would be thrown into complete disarray. As one officer put it when he learned that married quarters were to be privatised: "I don't want to sound snobbish but ..."

In the United States, General Colin Powell - the very same General Powell who wanted to kill the Iraqis - said that queers in the armed forces polarised attitudes. What he perhaps meant was that in the Army men were men and women were ... well, women. The distinction was not quite so clear-cut about the turn of the century. It has been reliably reported that a British general sent out to teach the Boers a lesson was, in fact, a woman. How he/she had managed to evade the MO for so long is one of those mysteries that enliven the conversation over port. At the very least, she must have had a well-controlled bladder. Winston Churchill, who was in South Africa as a subaltern at the time, may well have known about her. His own aversion to cross-dressers and queers came out in his treatment - as Home Secretary - of the Irish nationalist, Roger Casement. It's thought that Casement, a homosexual, might have escaped the death sentence had he been straight.

In Europe, attitudes in the armed forces have apparently polarised without any ill effects. Many countries, notably Denmark and Holland, tolerate homosexuals in the ranks. But then the Dutch probably learned a thing or two while administering their empire in the East. There's nothing like a few colonies to teach one the vagaries of human nature. The Danes also had a colonial fling. Wearing their funny little helmets with bulls' horns (a phallic symbol, if ever there was) and waving instruments of torture, they invaded England. They landed on the Kent coast not far from Canterbury, frightening the life out of the natives, who

45

thought it must be Sunday.

The Church of England has never been able to shake off the fancy dress or the nasty habits picked up from the Danes. To love one's brother in the Church of England has a meaning all of its own - which is probably why they beseech the Lord to lead them not into temptation. Many a parish priest, homo and hetero, has succumbed to the sinful lusts of the flesh and been summoned by the bishop to explain. Those churlish enough to plead that they were only taking the word of God literally have been defrocked. Others have had a kindly hand placed upon them. In Ireland, Catholic priests are tortured by lusts of their own. For hours, they sit in confessional boxes, listening to the sins of others. Everybody seems to be having a good time but themselves. Eventually, the strain becomes too much for them and they rush out to molest small boys and girls. The GOC Dublin, wearing his devil's helmet and waving a big stick adorned with the horns of BSE-resistant cattle, has told them to stop it, immediately. That sort of behaviour gives the church a bad name, even in Gaelic. The priests, speaking in Latin, have promised not to do it again.

But they will.

6

The not-so-ugly ducklings

Vita Sackville-West was once frightfully daring. On the way home to Sevenoaks, where the family had a small pad, she got off the train at Orpington and spent the night there with her girlfriend. Anybody who can squeeze a scintilla of romance out of Orpington must be not only a little odd but in the grip of the most fearful passion. The girlfriend in this case was Violet Trefusis, daughter of the King's mistress and, like Vita, a raging lesbian. What they did at Orpington is lost in the mists of time but it would probably have been more comfortable among the bracken in Knole Park.

Vita, the grand-daughter of a Spanish rag-and-bone merchant, was a big girl. She wore breeches at home and, in London, liked to dress up in men's clothes. Full of bravado, she used to walk down Piccadilly, giving a fairly good impression of Burlington Bertie, hoping that nobody would recognise her. In fact, she was probably hoping they would recognise her; there ain't much fun in anonymity, especially among the aristocracy. Moreover, she was doing little more than George Sand had done half a century earlier, except that Sand wasn't queer and dressed in men's clothes deliberately to outrage Parisian society.

Vita, daughter of the third Lord Sackville, was undoubtedly a beautiful woman, despite - or because of - her plebeian Spanish blood. The one thing that showed she was not like other gals was the pronounced down on her upper lip, the sort of thing that the marketing men in Gillette would like to get their hands on. (Strangely enough, the hero of Radclyffe Hall's novel, *The Well of Loneliness*, was also a big girl of good family.) But in the sexually-repressed atmosphere of the early 20th Century there was no chance of coming out. One could not discuss that sort of thing, even with one's mother. Vita's secret was known only to her husband, the homosexual Harold Nicolson, to a succession of lovers and to the deer in Knole Park who raised an inquisitive antler as she changed her clothes. She would go into the stables dressed as a boy and come out (that is to say, not come out) as the lady of the manor. One or two disreputable journalists in Fleet Street, who also happened to be lesbians, were, of course, in on the secret.

Across the Channel in France, to which Vita and Violet fled, pursued by their husbands, and where the fictional Stephen Morton of Radclyffe Hall's novel set up home with her lover, lived another pair of raging queers, Gertrude Stein and Alice Toklas. Like Vita and the fictional Stephen, Alice was a little hirsute. Gertrude was fat and ugly but had hair in the right places. Ernest Hemingway used to drink tea with them, straining it through his own moustache which proved that he was a 100 per cent, all-American boy. He had an extremely large ego and there was never any suggestion that the hero of *A Farewell to Arms* could possibly have been based upon him. Eventually, he threw up at the thought of what two old ladies might do in a double bed.

Gertrude probably became a lesbian because she was so ugly that no self-respecting man could even contemplate a little leg-over. In today's politically correct climate, her sexual preference would probably have been attributed to environmental, rather than genetic, factors. Alice, on the other hand, was a nice little thing; Jewish, of course, but none the worse for that. Together she and Gertrude kept the most celebrated artistic salon in Paris where true-blue painters like Picasso rubbed shoulders with composers like George Antheil and struggled to make sense of their host's amorphous ramblings. For Hemingway, the effort proved too much, causing him to bash his head against the nearest wall and to liberate Paris single-handedly at the end of the Second World War. He also evinced a strong dislike for lesbians, marrying four times.

Despite the fact that even Lady Sackville eventually twigged that Vita was having it off with Violet and that Virginia Woolf was not exactly Samantha Fox, there was a certain decorum about lesbian love in post-Edwardian Britain. It was truly the love that dared not speak its name, far removed from the messy, one-night stands associated with male homosexuality. Had Violet, Virginia or Vita been introduced to a saleslady from Ann Summers the story might have been rather different and the tower at Sissinghurst fitted out more imaginatively. Perhaps it was but as Vita was the only person allowed inside we shall never know. In any case, the 3Vs were tremendous snobs and would never have associated with anybody who thought the old school tie was a form of bondage.

Vita herself was 'liberated' by Violet Keppel (as she then was) during a passionate weekend at Long Barn, Vita's home near Sevenoaks, in April 1918. Harold was away chasing boys on the Continent while up in Michigan Ernest was being hailed as a hero for stopping a bullet on the Italian front. The fictional Stephen and her lover were driving ambulances somewhere in the mud. Stephen's creator, Radclyffe Hall, was living openly with a woman in London although her book was not to see the light of day for 30 years. Along with *Ulysses* and *La Terre*, it was condemned by the censor as unfit for human consumption and banned. Compared with Vita's true-life romance with the volcanic Violet, *The Well of Loneliness* is pretty tame stuff. But, at the time, it took a brave woman to commit such thoughts to paper.

Now they have the freedom to publish whatever they like the liberated lesbians of the nineties simply will not shut up. The demand equal rights, equal space in the newspapers to promote their views, equal time on air to denounce men and show the world how to get along without them. What they should be doing - and quietly, at that - is doing whatever lesbians do. Most women are not interested in their genetically bent sisters. They like men and dream of nothing better than being strapped to a bed and raped by a dark-skinned stranger. (Ask the market researchers.) They will strip off to entertain the crowds at Wimbledon or Twickenham and pose naked in front of a camera, especially if it helps to sell newspapers and put a few pennies in their own pockets. Sexual freedom, after all, includes the freedom to have one's own bank account. Only the strident viragos of the feminist movement - many of them battered wives and unloved lesbians - insist that the poor things are being exploited. Perhaps they are but it is with their consent.

Nobody forces the female of the species to stand in front of a camera to advertise sun glasses or to show that eating ice cream can be exciting. They do so because they like the work and, even more so, the rewards. The rewards include being taken out to dinner by a rich old Greek and gently seduced afterwards. If one were to object, word would get around and a girl would have to buy her own dinner. It is self-evident, therefore, that girls who survive on Luncheon Vouchers, either because of their principles or because their breath smells, are going to complain the loudest about exploitation of the female form. What do they think the old gentleman had in mind? A discussion about democratic socialism?

There is, of course, the ever present danger of rape. Rape is seduction without consent and it worries lesbians and feminists a great deal. They have a sneaking suspicion that some of the victims may be protesting too much. In one of Scott Fitzgerald's short stories, a well-brought-up young lady is heard to complain about rape. Yes, she exclaimed breathlessly, it was rape, rape, rape all summer long. Lucky old thing! In these politically correct times, however, it is not good form to admit that a little rape now and again is better than reliance on alcohol or valium. Rape is a violation of the inalienable rights of women and God knows what else in the hands of an American lawyer. Even a British lawyer can expand his vocabulary by adding all the right phrases from feminist trash sheets to make a wholly natural pursuit sound like the invasion of Genghis Khan. Provided that adequate precautions are taken (e.g., the pill beforehand), an unexpected and close encounter of the sexual kind can restore the bloom to a middle-aged maiden's cheek.

It goes without saying that those who clog up the courts with their allegations of rape tend to be members of the lower classes. How often does one hear of a duchess complaining that she had been taken unawares by a complete stranger while strolling in the grounds of a country house, somewhere in England? It is precisely to encourage such encounters that the owners of such homes invite guests for weekend, and why the guests accept. As Noel Coward observed, the stately homes of England have seen more than one poor little rich girl being beastly to the Germans. Of course, what Aldous Huxley described as the 'Malthusian drill' is even more vital now that HIV is rampant among the genes of the nobility. But AIDS is a small price to pay for the pleasure of doing what comes naturally to everyone but the Getrude Steins of this world.

Some people have done very well out of feminist and lesbian claptrap. There are specialist publishers for ladies who prefer to sleep standing up; pubs, clubs and gay bars for ladies who prefer to meet and lie down; and personal columns for shy little girls with moustaches and a Manet in the bedroom. But the biggest beneficiaries have undoubtedly been the lawyers and those who administer sex discrimination law.

Just imagine the trouble that poor old Kit Marlowe would have had with the Equal Opportunities Commission had it existed when he penned the innocent lines in *Macbeth:* 'How now, you secret, black and midnight hags!' The law would have been on to him in a flash. What do you mean by calling my client a hag? Are you implying that she is not physically well-endowed and is likely to strike fear and loathing into the hearts of all decent men? And what do mean by secret? Are you suggesting that she is a member of the Mafia, smuggling drugs under cover of darkness? As for black, m'lud, this scribbler is guilty of the most blatant racial prejudice.

What would Bessie Braddock have made of it all? She was, as Churchill reminded her late one evening, as ugly as sin and likely to remain that way. Three hundred years earlier, she could well have passed as the original midnight hag.

Oh, God! We have no Bananas!

Following the death of Vita Sackville-West in 1962, the tower at Sissinghurst, which had been her intensely private domain, was for the first time exposed to the vulgar gaze of the public. There, among the knick-knacks of a literary lady who lived apart from her husband, was found a battered leather case. The lock was rusty and the key missing, suggesting at first that it might have been some form of medieval chastity belt. When forced, several volumes of poetry by the French homosexual and poet Paul Verlaine fell out. Verlaine - the subject of her husband's first biography - had himself fallen out with his lover, the poet and gun-runner Jean Rimbaud, over whom should spend the housekeeping money. The following scrap, scribbled hastily on what appeared to be a badly-printed copy of the Sevenoaks Chronicle, was found wedged in the spine of *Romances sans Paroles*. While most of Vita's works have been pawed over by scholars for many years, this extract - which shows that political correctness had already begun to sap the intellectual vigour of the nation - is reproduced here for the first time. Exclusively.

June 21, 1930. Midsummer! How glorious the garden looks with all the weeds H. brought back from Teheran. I'm sure he's fundamentally correct in saying that one day cannabis will grow wild in the hedgerows. O, if only we could change the botanical face of Britain! Our talk on the wireless the other day has caused quite a sensation. Apparently, the hoi polloi thought marriage was about sex and the inevitable consequences of it. I'm glad we put them right. I can't say I like C. [Cyril Connolly]. He reminds me too much of the weeds. I rather think that Dr. Stopes ought to have had a quiet word with his parents. Thoughtless coupling only propels the world towards demographic disaster.

O, how I wish Violet were here! If not Violet, then Mary. Harold, dear, sweet man that he is, always makes me feel lonely. I need a woman. I don't really care who she is so long as it's not some little bedint who will sell our story to the News of the World. Ethel Smyth told me she had been having trouble with the paparazzi. I can well believe it although I do not fancy Ethel myself. Her masculinity makes me afraid of what might happen to Virginia (with any luck).

We have a Labour government; for how long, I wonder? I fear that, like marriage, the honeymoon will soon be over. Two weeks, two months? We shall see. The man MacDonald is frightfully bedint although he wears his clothes well. Sometimes he reminds me of Dada and if he came here [to Knole] I'm sure the deer would respect him, even in the rutting season. None of the Cabinet seems to know much about women. If only one of them would marry a KC there might be a glimmer of hope. I do wish I could come out and say this openly, instead of having to confide it to my diary.

Harold is going back to Berlin in a couple of days. That horrible little bedint, Herr Schicklgruber (the one with the moustache), is going to make trouble, I know. He has already threatened to burn down the Reichstag, but not before filling it with Jews, gypsies and transvestites. Beware! Christopher [Isherwood] wrote the other day, predicting that he might have to say goodbye to Berlin. This will break his heart as he has ein schlusslicht there. Not for the first time the lights are going out all over Europe.

I have been wondering why women found Byron so attractive. He was beautiful, yes, but so are a lot of men. There must have been something else about him. Reputation, perhaps? Would I, like Augusta, have singed my wings? I fear that I might. There is a mystery about Lord B. that, I suspect, will only be solved by opening his tomb and having a look. I'm not the prurient type myself but am sure it could be arranged. Will have a word with the people at Longleat (or is it Long Ford? I can never remember.).

I do wish Harold would hurry up and go back to Berlin. He makes me nervous. Conjugal bliss is not supposed to last more than a week at a time and then only if it cannot be avoided. I can never understand why Harold said he wanted to kill Violet. To hate is all very well and the natural corollary of passion. But to kill indicates a lack of finer feelings. I thought I had married a gentleman; now I'm not so sure. I'm glad that Dada was a lord and that even the King has to make do with fewer rooms than ourselves. It's a pity that we have to pay tax and HM does not.

Now that we have a Labour government, the servants are becoming bolshie. I hope they will not go on strike. One of them, I'm sure, deliberately sewed buttons down the front of my breeches to make me look like a man. If I can identify the culprit, I will send him (or her) to Malaga to research Grandmama's family. He (or she) will soon learn that Spain is no place for Bolsheviks.

I was rather taken by the little piece at the BBC who produced our talk on the radio. When I can get rid of Harold, and shake off Rosamund, Virginia, Mary et al., I must get to know her better. It is only by suborning people in positions of power and influence that we of the twilight sex will be able to bend genders to our own satisfaction. It may not be politically correct to say so but it is so.

The man Halpern is coming to tea so must remember to buy some bananas. Apparently, he ...(The manuscript breaks off at this point.)

Dr Mohamed Chunda Singh, consultant psychiatrist and chronicler of the Bloomsbury set, has studied the document and writes:

The fragment we have seen above is not sufficient to paint a portrait of a marriage but it does provide a useful snapshot. Clearly, the lady in question is suffering from penis envy. Her repressed sexuality manifests itself in every sentence. There is no doubt she hates her husband and would like to kill him. This would leave her free to conduct illicit love affairs with her women friends, including the person referred to as Virginia. The first two syllables of this name are, in my opinion, most significant. That she sees this creature as some sort of vestal virgin is self-evident. She is not afraid of Virginia but would like to protect her; perhaps even to dominate her. In time, the vestal nature of the relationship will give way to lust.

The reference to Byron is intriguing. She more or less admits that should would like to have been laid by this scourge of the upper classes whose treatment of women, including his own sister, was nothing short of scandalous. It is entirely significant that one of the early poems by this lame womaniser was entitled *Childe Harold*. This was the name of her very own husband - a man who, by all accounts, had never really grown up and whom she could not pack off to the war zone quickly enough. I have often come across women displaying this duality of personality. They pretend to be homosexual, mainly to choke off unwanted suitors, such as small men with moustaches and large men with insatiable carnal appetites. But secretly, in the Tower or wherever they are confined, they fantasise about the real men of this world. Such, I suspect, was the case with Byron (or Mr Longy, as I have sometimes heard him called).

Like many wealthy women, she longed to suffer at the hands of the working class. Hence her reference to the new Labour government and the amount of tax her family paid. I have no wish to draw a Freudian conclusion but it is obvious that she was crying out to be whipped by men in cloth caps. She herself may be worn such clothing on occasion and even indulged in self-flagellation. The decision to send a servant to Spain to mingle with the masses is simply a ploy to obtain vicarious sexual pleasure.

Perhaps the most telling point is that the foregoing document was found wedged in the spine of Verlaine. I do not know much about this gentleman myself, except that he was queer and had spent some time in prison for wounding his lover. I fear it is the old, old story of the green-eyed monster - in this case, penis envy - giving rise to passions that cannot be assuaged by normal means. It is terribly, terribly sad that this poor woman could not come to terms with her sexuality.

But now she is dead does it really matter?

7

Hop off, you frogs

Le frogs - that is to say, the race of snail eaters who live on the wrong side of the English Channel - are typical of the foreigners who infest the Continent. More than once have the British had to send the cream of their youth - some in uniform, some in football-club strips - to sort them out. But the frogs never learn. They continue to regard les anglais as uncivilised barbarians - the sort of people who would erect a glass pyramid on the centre court at Wimbledon. The French, on the other hand, are - are everyone except the editors of scurrilous tabloid newspapers knows perfectly well - God's chosen people (after the Jews, that is).

The frogs, who are essentially a nation of apple growers and grape treaders, suffer from a folie de grandeur which stems from the fact that they once had an empire. Not quite as big as the British empire, of course, and a different colour (usually green) on the maps of the world. (Very small maps, known as the *Guide Michelin*, are sometimes coloured blue.) Moreover, the frogs have never really got over the loss of Canada and the Louisiana delta. Had the southern states of America remained in French hands, towns such as St Louis and New Orleans would be filled with Arabs from North Africa and not slaves from East Africa. This would have allowed people to attend the Cannes film festival without being forced to lie on the cobblestones making the beast with two backs. In Muraroa atoll in the South Pacific (props: Mr Rodgers and Mr Hammerstein), beasts with two backs, three eyes and very often no arms or legs are a common feature of the environment, thanks to French civilisation.

In addition to their empire, the frogs were also well endowed with thinkers, such as Jean-Paul Sartre, who invented existentialism. Nobody really knew what existentialism meant and, as M. Sartre is now dead, it's doubtful if anybody ever will know. But it was certainly a good thing while it lasted, showing the value of education and making a fortune for M. Sartre and his mistress, Simone de Beauvoir. Mlle. de Beauvoir is also dead, alas. The great thing about both of them was that, during their lifetimes, all those who agreed with them - especially the students at the Sorbonne who manned the barricades during the riots of 1968 - were politically correct. Anybody who disagreed, or was too thick to grasp the meaning of existentialism, was politically incorrect. The p.i.s. included senior officers in the Army who were so confused they sent a man with a little plastique to clear the air. The resulting explosion wrecked M. Sartre's apartment but did little to improve understanding. In the orchards of Normandie, the clash between the might of the armed forces and the blight of existentialism later became known as le crunch.

Indeed, it was a bunch of frogs - the du Ponts - who, ignoring the fact that Baton Rouge had been sold to Spain, moved to America and set up a factory for making gunpowder. The Chinese had relinquished the patent and the formula was up for grabs. In due course, the du Ponts supplied ammunition to everyone who wanted to fight, thus making a fortune and establishing a dynasty in the state of de la war. To show how even-handed they were, and how the freedom to make money need not be compromised by any misplaced feelings of fraternity, they even supplied the Germans. Nobody understands the Germans, mainly because of their old-fashioned writing and incredibly complicated compound nouns. But there is no doubt they are superior to the French, except in matters of intellect, and will one day provide a king, as well as a currency, for the whole of Europe.

The Germans have always been politically correct, even when they were wrong. They were certainly wrong to start the first world war and probably wrong to start the second. They were undoubtedly right to lose both contests as this has made them the strongest country in Europe, peopled by superior beings known as Young Turks. There are many millions of Turks in Germany, making Mercedes Benz and teaching soccer hooligans how to throw hand grenades back at the British. Middle-class Germans spend their time drinking beer and complaining about the price of Danish butter. In recent times, they have begun to complain about beef; in particular, British beef. Since the end of the war (global, mark II), the Germans have eaten more beef than anybody. This has made them fat but it was only when they stopped making beetles did anyone realise it was also driving them mad. An early indication that all was not well came in 1960 when President John F Kennedy peered over the Berlin wall and announced that he was a doughnut (ich bien ein Berliner). He was put down the following year. But it was not until a British prime minister began to exhibit bovine tendencies that the World Health Organisation realised it had an epidemic on its hands. All cattle were rounded up and put in a big oven. The Jews decided to let bygones be bygones and stopped selling beef sandwiches at Marx et Spencer. This allowed everybody to concentrate on the war in Bosnia and provided the intellectual frisson missing from the international scene since the death of Monsieur Sartre.

The French and the Germans have one overwhelming advantage in the modern world. Apart from those with slinky eyes or Turkish surnames, most of them are white. This sets them apart from other foreigners, many of whom are black (although it is not politic to mention the fact, unless in a positive way). The former U.S. Chief of Staff, General Powell, is black, although many of those who served under him may once have been members of the Klu Klux Klan. It is therefore politically incorrect to refer to the heroes of Iraq as black bastards although it is perfectly all right to describe civilian looters as such.

Nor are bastards always black. An exasperated colonel in the U.N. force trying to keep the peace in Yugoslavia described Serbs, Croats and Bosnians alike as 'all bloody bastards'. This may not have been diplomatic but it was certainly the truth. There are plenty of white bastards around, including some in the Conservative Party. And one must not forget the little yellow bastards whose own delusions of grandeur were only stopped by le poudre du Pont in 1945. The Japanese - lest one is trying to think of what sort of bastards they might be - are now a peaceful little race of geisha girls and sumo wrestlers, with a handful of corrupt politicians, bent bankers and unsuccessful copper traders on the side. It is, of course, not polite to mention Japanese peccadilloes in public, especially if one is hoping to do business with a failed kamikaze pilot who plans to build a factory in Britain. One radio announcer in Tyne and Wear was invited to commit hara kiri after a careless remark about the little yellow investors bringing employment to the region.

The strange habits of the average foreigner have always been a butt for jokes. Poles and Italians are usually at the receiving end, in the absence of a handy Red Indian or wog. But the disgusting habits of primitive peoples can also be a source of concern at a cultural level. As far back as 1913, long before the BBC had even thought of Panorama, the British Board of Film Censors was worried about the learning difficulties of people who sat in the back rows of the newly-built (and dimly-lit) silent-picture houses. It therefore decreed that any film depicting 'native customs in foreign lands abhorrent to British ideas' must not be shown. So much for David Attenborough.

But one never knows what foreigners will do. In West Irian (the wrong half of New Guinea), the authorities have been forced to clamp down on the old native custom of walking about naked. It was thought in Djakarta that too much flesh might frighten away tourists. As the only reason for going to West Irian is to see such flesh, the directive to wear clothes is hard to understand. In any case, male West Irians (who only 20 years ago used to eat tourists for breakfast) are not naked. They wear fetching gourds over their penis to keep away the flies. At times of sexual excitement, the gourds can flick suddenly upwards, inflicting a nasty injury on any passing Violet or Virginia. Perhaps for this reason alone the government has decided that a pair of ex-Army jungle shorts might be safer.

It is not only in West Irian that the habits of primitive people cause anger and indignation. In Saudi Arabia, for instance, the custodians of Islam punish criminals and maintain feminine hygiene by cutting off various parts of the body. In serious cases, involving members of the royal family or adultery, the whole head is removed. Thieves and minor wrongdoers escape with the loss of a hand. Mere women - at last count, several million of them - are deprived of sexual pleasure by having their clitoris lopped. To lose this vital part of the body it is not necessary to commit any crime at all; merely to think of a loved one. Unlike public executions, which are often show on television, the operation is usually carried out in private to avoid antagonising loud-mouthed western women. Unless one wishes to lose a contract, however, one does not accuse the Saudis of feudal barbarism. Nor does one mention the American record in such matters; doctors in the United States used to do exactly the same thing to stop women 'abusing' themselves. Foreigners are all the same, really.

The Saudis may be feudal but they have a very effective way of dealing with drug pedlars. They behead them, like common princesses. The Malays, also Moslem, hang them by the neck until dead. Years ago, when the Shah ruled Persia, the Iranians did the same. The Chinese simply put offenders against the nearest wall and shot them. All these simple, cheap and effective ways of putting drug dealers out of business are ignored by the West or written off as too horrible to contemplate. The British Prime Minister, John Major, even interceded (admittedly, just before a crucial by-election) on behalf of convicted drug smugglers in Thailand. Who knows?; the drug dealer of today could be the president of Panama or Columbia tomorrow. Those bestial Saudis would not give them a chance.

While the Saudis are still feeling their way through the quicksands of political correctness, the British are old hands at the game - thanks to their empire. The empire was full of foreigners: abos, boongs, wogs, chinks - even the half-bred chee-chee of that illustrious jewel in the crown, India. The message from London, relayed by the World Service, was essentially the same: we are right and you are wrong. (This message was later refined and adopted by the BBC which took over the World Service.) The master had a simple way of correcting the views of natives who had wobbled off course; they were hung, shot or beaten with flails until the confessed the error of their ways. Many an insurrection that could have been put down over a quiet drink at the Residency was turned into a full-scale revolt by a display of stiff upper lips. Once the corrective process was over, normal drinking was resumed.

The efficacy of the colonial system is best illustrated by the current dearth of aborigines in Australia. When the first fleet arrived, there were probably about a million abos wandering about, stark naked, and enticing the lads from the hulks with offers of gin. (This turned out to be the first misunderstanding: gin is merely the aboriginal word for woman.) Moreover, the native inhabitants of this huge sheep run seemed to be under the impression that the land belonged to them, even though there were no fences or boundary posts. Very often, they threw primitive spears at the interlopers who, for some reason, dragged leg-irons through the bush. Eventually, the British (who, by this time, included a young lad named Ned Kelly) had to show who was boss and put down nearly all the abos in a diabolical display of political correctness. That's why today there are only a judge and a couple of abo poets left.

Eventually, of course, the old lags managed to slough off the shackles of empire and assume the mantle of indigenes themselves. It was then that they began to have trouble with foreigners. The first were the chinks who could smell gold from a million miles. Junkloads of them arrived, mainly in Queensland, and began scrambling over rocks and gullies in search of the yellow metal. They had an unfortunate habit of working harder than the ex-convicts and members of the upper classes who had joined the rush. They had to be taught a lesson. They were. Permits to dig became harder to obtain. They were robbed, beaten and their shacks set on fire. One little chap was nailed to a tree by his ears. The following day the bucket on which he stood was kicked away. The Chinese took the hint and left the goldfields to open restaurants.

But then the Australians discovered they had no-one to work on the sugar plantations. This was back-breaking work, hardly suitable for a white man. So, as machines had not been invented, they had to import large black men from the South Seas who were used to standing in the sun all day. For the islanders, it was an educative process. As an early Queenslander explained, they probably benefited from the experience. It was, however, not so beneficial for the plantation owners of Fiji who, finding themselves short of labour, had to import workers from India. There was no shortage there as the Indians were not then practising vasectomy. Nor, as it turned out, were the Kanakas in Queensland. After a few years, there were so many of them that they had to be expelled. To make it all legal and above board, the Australians introduced the White Australia Act. This allowed Greeks to open milk bars in Melbourne while ensuring that the moral fibre of the nation was not undermined by large black men swinging hoes. The Act was only repealed after the second world war when the Australians (and New Zealanders) feared they might need allies to counter French colonial attitudes in the South Pacific.

Ironically, both the French and the Greeks now find themselves more or less on the same side in Europe where the post-colonial misfits tend to speak English. In recent years, the politically correct way to deal with anything emanating from Brussels has been to stand on the cliffs at Dover and hurl abuse. Like the boomerang, however, the abuse often misses its target and comes straight back, hitting the abuser in the neck. That's why so many Conservative Members of Parliament are sceptical that anything will ever be achieved by shouting at foreigners. They simply don't understand.

8

How green was my welly?

The Romans had a nice line in road-building. They tied a yellow ribbon around the leg of an old crow and told it to fly to Chester, where carrion awaited. The crow, thinking only of its stomach, took off and flew there in a straight line. Half a dozen centurions, marching at breakneck pace, followed it over hill and dale, stopping only to crack a few locals over the head with their theodolites. The locals, with nothing to wear but woad, were not a pretty sight. They had long hair and a truculent attitude. Viewed against the setting sun, the blue of their dermatological blight should have produced a restful shade of green. Instead, it only gave rise to aural pollution which was later set to music and called the Motorway Blues.

The crow eventually reached its destination and was rewarded, not with the promised carrion, but with an idiom, or clichè. The centurions arrived shortly afterwards, only slightly out of breath and covered in mud. Even in those days, crows preferred to fly over areas of outstanding natural beauty and not grotty urban streets with pavements. Had the Romans been more observant, they might have noticed that the route took them through colonies of prehistoric snails. But they saw nothing, apart from trees that would have to be cut down and huge rocks that had clearly fallen off the back of a lorry on the way to Stonehenge. The word from Rome was that the empire had to be secured, no matter how many illiterate oiks were evicted from their hovels or snails crushed underfoot.

In the centuries that followed, nobody was quite able to replicate the Roman idea of following the crow. Indeed, during the 16th and 17th Centuries, the Michelin Guide replaced the abstemious Romans with the rolling English drunkard. The drunkard had no idea where he was going and often ended up in the river. But at least he peed in the hedgerows and was no threat to the environment. Even his ale was brewed naturally, with hops and barley and things like that. He was essentially a harmless creature, never happier than when quaffing a pint or telling a passing Roman how to take the scenic route to Aqua Vitae. He thus became the earliest known example of the environmentally-friendly Englishman: a lost soul at peace with the world and in complete harmony with his surroundings, especially if he had missed the river and ended up in the pigsty.

It was only when the road builders of the late 20th Century discovered that the rolling English road caused bottlenecks (what else?) that they reinstated the Roman idea of following the crow. Unfortunately, most crows had by now been domesticated and flew around in circles to bypass the snails and thwart the men with theodolites. In fury, the hard-hatted ones responded with an outbreak of idiomatic English that reverberated throughout the countryside. Eventually, peace was restored and the crows encouraged to fly round in ever-decreasing circles until, hopefully, they disappeared. It had nevertheless been established that while straight roads were probably the shortest way between two points, they were not necessarily the quickest. The friends of the environment, including the rolling English drunkard, had again won the day.

The Romans were extremely lucky, of course, that they had only roads to build and not nuclear power plants to decommission or obsolete oil platforms to sink in the North Sea. Nor did they have to dispose of sewage in a manner that would earn them a blue flag of convenience from the chief legionnaire in Brussels. They were, however, environmentally conscious, mainly because deodorants propelled by cfc's had not been invented. Had they been told by the hairy Norsemen who peered through the mist at the sceptered isle that smoke from the fires under their baths was damaging the pinewoods in Hafrsfjord they might have reduced the temperature. But as nobody had been to public school they simply pulled out the plug and let the hot water escape down the Bristol Channel. As the bath superintendent remarked at the time: "When in Britannia, do as the barbarians do." The oysters on Lundy Island quite enjoyed the experience for a while but became allergic to soap suds and moved to Wales.

The Norsemen who cast such covetous eyes on Britannia had no idea of the non-marine riches that lay beneath the waves. There was sludge, it's true, but that could not easily be turned into brass. The only oil they knew about came in bottles and was forced down their throats in childhood. (That is why they grew up to be such strapping lads.) Not until somebody invented the motor car were they persuaded to take a crash course in geology. They discovered there was brass under the waves after all - and in their very own backyard. When the barbarians across the water decided to pull out yet another plug - this time, the bung keeping the Brent Spar oil platform afloat - the hairy ones jumped up and down, chanting 'Not in our backyard'. The cry was adopted by everyone who wanted to be politically correct on environmental issues.

The argument over what can and cannot be dumped in other people's backyards is at the heart of the environmental debate. Even to define other people's backyards when Martians drop their unwanted fossils on the planet is very difficult. Ironically, the traditional method of waste disposal - over the side and into the sea - is favoured by both sides of the environmental divide. Those charged with keeping the streets clean or dispensing with spent nuclear fuel rods say the method is cheap and effective. The shareholders like it and so does the Treasury because it helps to keep down public spending. Without a handy ocean, local authorities would have to acquire land or build expensive treatment plants and that would only put up taxes. The opponents of land-fill, who would prefer the fish rather than themselves to suffer, agree. They say that salt water is an ideal way to sterilise needles infected with HIV. This method has, in fact, proved very effective in sterilising the ocean itself. Off the coast of Maine and Rhode Island, hardly anything moves of its own volition. This saves an awful lot of trouble over fishing quotas: no fish, so why argue? Even the waters between England and Ireland provide an ideal solution for diluting old mustard gas. Millions of tons of dodgy ammunition have been dumped there, not far from the new gas pipeline. This could one day throw an entirely new light on the theory of global warming. But, as the ammo dumpers pointed out, we were there first and, anyway, it's our backyard, not yours.

Public perceptions are changing, however. There is a politically correct way to deal with the environment and an incorrect way. The correct way of persuading the Greenpeace Warrior to sail into the sunset was to have a quiet word with the skipper. Instead, a couple of French non-so-secret agents blew it up - or, rather, sank it in Auckland harbour. This put the frogs in a bad light and raised doubts over their commitment to libertè and fraternitè. The official excuse was that the agents had been searching for a new type of mollusc, found only on the hulls of environmental protection vessels in the southern hemisphere. Owing to a water-logged code book, they thought that 'attendez le limpet' meant attach a mine. Such is the danger of double-speak. The agents, a man and a woman, were sent to a small island with eight records and a plentiful supply of champagne while the PR men in Paris tried to put a spin on their predicament.

The need to explain environmental decisions in a user-friendly way presents the p.c. lobby with one of its biggest challenges. Companies take great care not to upset their customers and reflect their concern for the environment with words, as well as action. The desire to be politically correct, influenced by the effect of public opinion on paraffin sales, encouraged the Shell oil company to abandon plans to sink the Brent Spar in the North Sea. It also gave rise to a prize example of how p.c. distorts the language. On the very day that the company's detractors apologised for getting their 'facts' wrong, the Energy Minister, Tim Eggar, coined a new word to describe the ecological impact of dumping toxic waste at sea. There were, he said, a number of 'disbenefits'. This would not have been out of place in 1984 when double-speak was at least explicable. Of course, Mr Eggar may have meant disadvantages - but in any non-Orwellian thesaurus of English words and phrases that has negative connotations. In politics, one must always remain positive, especially when faced with the potential loss of corporation and sales tax.

Could there also be disbenefits to privatising nuclear power stations or selling state-owned woodlands? The new owners might cut down all the broad-leaved natural species and plant acres and acres of fast-growing cupressus. Evidence shows that this practice not only drives out the red squirrel but causes osprey and eagles to lose their way. Twitchers have to be installed to help them find their nests. And what about the rhododendron disfiguring the landscape of Snowdonia? These rampant, free-flowering shrubs were imported from the Himalayas in the 19th Century and have since taken over the backyards of country houses everywhere. The only way to get rid of them is to apply for a grant from the European Union and spray them with herbicide. This does, however, give rise to a number of disbenefits, including the fact that Snowdon looks better clothed in pink rhododendron than in its natural, barren state.

Hughie Batchelor, a crotchety old farmer in Kent, had a very similar idea for dealing with unwanted vegetation. He decided it was far more profitable to grub out hedgerows and claim a subsidy from Brussels than waste time trimming them with a pair of scissors every year. Down came the hedges, out went the birds, badgers and courting couples and in rolled the cheques. Hughie was told that, to preserve the landscape known to generations of rolling English drunkards, he had to stop. He didn't and was put in jail. But he was only doing what comes naturally when

Brussels encourages anti-social behaviour. He was politically correct but environmentally wrong. Only death put an end to his subsidies.

From hedgerows to ballast water may not seem a natural progression but in the sphere of environmental protection it is one that could soon put nitrogenous fertilisers in the shade. Ballast water - the stuff that keeps tankers steady when there is no oil to carry - is not exactly the nectar of the gods. Nor does it come from pure mountain streams, bordered by rhododendron, that in modern India are somewhat hard to find. Very often, it is indistinguishable from bilge water - except that it doesn't taste as sweet. It is, of course, racially offensive to suggest that raw sewage from one continent is more lethal than that from another. Suffice it to say that some ships, after discharging their cargo in Calcutta, refill their tanks with the local brew. This has been shown - by totally objective, non-racial analysis - to contain every germ known to mankind. It may also contain one or two dead rats harbouring the plague and the remains of several funeral pyres along the Lower Ganges. When the ship arrives at its next destination, often in the Mediterranean, the temporary cargo of typhus and yellow fever is discharged into the sea. The captain is not breaking any law because the mixture is only water, not crude oil which would spoil the beaches. But next to swimming alongside a disused Russian submarine under the polar ice cap a mouthful of this stuff is probably the quickest way to Paradise. And yet ones does not hear much about it because to single out Calcutta staphylococci would imply racial discrimination and detract attention from the proposed motorway.

As Tim Eggar demonstrated, the politically-alert minister has always to look on the positive side. Peasants whose hovels are about to be demolished to make way for the Channel Tunnel must be given the facts so that they can make an informed choice: either to get out or have trainloads of frogs gesticulating as you go to the bathroom. Those who live near the motorway should be informed of the benefits (not the disbenefits) of having one's own transport - so important when the buses aren't running. On no account should a minister be drawn into a discussion on the BBC about the beneficial effects of car-free days in Athens or Los Angeles. This would only cause panic and depress the shares of oil companies and car manufacturers. Far better to say nothing and let visiting pop stars wear smog masks when they arrive in London on a perfectly clear day.

The late Lord Brabazon, former chairman of the British Overseas Airways Corporation, was not one to suffer euphemisms gladly. He had never heard of political correctness or of the need to adjust one's Press statement before voicing it in public. When told there were objections to lengthening the runway at Heathrow, he declared that the profits of his airline were more important than the comfort of a few peasants who happened to live in West London.

Lord Brabazon had an aeroplane named after him; it was such a disaster that it failed to get off the ground. As an exponent of political correctness, Lord Brabazon was also a disaster. He would never have made the grade in any of George Orwell's novels and clearly didn't have a green welly in the house. It's a pity he died before the outbreak of mad word disease.

8a

Without the Rice

Good morning! This is your soothsayer, Captain Malthus, speaking. Please tighten your belts as we are about to enter a hot-air zone and you may experience some gastronomic turbulence.

You may have noticed at breakfast that you were served only muesli and natural spring water. This will have come as a shock to those of you brought up on kedgeree and devilled kidneys. But for most people in the Third World a plate of muesli is more than they get during the course of an entire week.

I don't want to sound moralistic about this - I'm a sky pilot, not a politician - but some of you, especially those who shop at Sainsburys and travel club class, have always had it too good. I regret to say that the wind of change is blowing ominously in your direction.

On arrival at Heathrow, you will notice that the runway has been ploughed up to provide extra rations for refugees from Hungary. This might make the landing a bit bumpy but that's something you'll have to get used to. Before the decade is out, we're all going to be hungry. In fact, we shall probably starve to death.

Quite frankly, the population is growing at an alarming rate. There are far too many mouths to feed and not enough land. By 1980 (and this concerns all of us, not just members of the Mile High Club), there will be standing room only. Most of you here today will be gone by the mid-seventies. Those who survive will be under-nourished and poverty-stricken.

Moreover, natural resources are running out. The coal mines won't last for ever, despite what Mr Scargill says, and we cannot rely on wind farms and one or two oilfields under the North Sea. Even uranium will be of little help. You can't eat plutonium or exchange it for worldly goods. The Russians know that only too well.

Some of you may think I'm being unduly pessimistic. After all, the prophets of doom have been wrong before. But I have in front of me a calculation which shows that, unless we can bribe farmers to grow more food, we shall die of starvation - unless, of course, we die of something else. I have a feeling that some form of divine retribution - perhaps the long-promised plague - is at hand.

The question is: what form will the pestilence take? Will it be just a few locusts which devour the remaining crops? Or will it be a plague of Biblical proportions that strikes down the young and gay (or as gay as it's possible to be on the verge of death)? I fear it could well be the latter.

Don't get me wrong: I'm not trying to predict the future or put the fear of God into you. But we at Doomwatch Airways have already noticed a large hole in the ozone layer over the Falklands. It's true that not many people could say where the Falklands were or to whom they belong. But we ignore these warnings at our peril. The Falklands today, Gibraltar tomorrow - if, indeed, there is to be a tomorrow.

The prophets of doom can't all be wrong - so make the most of your muesli and collect your Rewards while you can. In the world of the future, you will be foraging among the hedgerows for a few stinging nettles to assuage the pangs of hunger.

On behalf of Doomwatch Airways, I should like to thank you for putting up with this diatribe and hope that you have a nice day, a decent lunch and a better tomorrow. We apologise for any discomfort that may have been caused.

Will passengers for Sodom and Gomorrah please remain on the aircraft until all health formalities have been completed? Thank you.

9

The mink, I think

Odd, isn't it, that four little words - which imply choice and the fruits of an enterprise culture - should be so charged with political incorrectness? The mere thought of adorning the shoulders of a beautiful woman with the pelts of dead animals is anathema to vegetarians and meat-eaters alike. In the world of p.c., fur is verboten. It is no longer chic to be seen at the opera wearing a mink coat, a sable stole or even the brush from a mangy old fox that failed to outrun a few hounds. To be fashionable, the politically-correct lady has to brave the chill winter nights in a synthetic garment - a fun fur - that will attract the plaudits of animal lovers and the sneers of the Old Guard, who are not going to give up the real stuff for anybody, even Brigitte Bardot. Especially Brigitte Bardot.

Ever since Wilde penned a witty line about English gentlemen pursuing the tinker's lunch, the politically correct have been getting hot under the collar about animal rights. A few seals clubbed to death while a television crew is on the same ice floe is guaranteed to raise a storm of protest. The clubbers - who are essentially no different to the knife men in an abattoir who cut the mad bits out of ancient dairy cows - have to justify their actions. We are, they invariably explain, culling the seals for their own benefit. Better a dead seal than no room on the ice floe for the next TV crew who happen along. Nothing is said about all the fish they eat or the disease they spread after bathing in ballast water. No, the seals are clubbed - just as old people in China were clubbed to death - to release their souls. Do seals have souls? The question adds a metaphysical dimension to the debate on animal rights.

Given the choice, most seals would probably try to avoid the premature release of their souls until ready to make that last journey to the great fish pond in the sky. Mink are of the same opinion, happy to roam about the prairie until stumbling into a hunter's trap. This is a far, far better way to go than waiting for death cooped up like a beakless battery hen. English foxes, which in the past liked nothing better than a good romp in the hen house, are today not so sure; easy living has made them morally ambivalent. Their natural haunt - the countryside - is fraught with danger. The waterholes are polluted and the natives unfriendly. The towns are much safer, with more food and less chance of being chewed up by a pack of bloodthirsty hounds. Moreover, towns contain people whose antipathy to hunting is imbued with a class hatred upon which mangy old foxes thrive.

In the pink corner are the huntsmen, and women, as politically incorrect as it's possible to be outside the polling booth (inside of which they're usually true blue). In the red, or green, corner are the assorted anarchists, unemployed paint sprayers and tremulous housewives who see it as their duty to protect the little foxes. (Of course, we all know that their real aim is to prevent the toffs having fun on horseback.) Ironically, the real punch-ups on the hunting field occur not between huntsmen and saboteurs - the disruptive ones have learned to avoid the whipper-in - but among those who rely on the gentry for a living. The foxes are well aware of this - which is why they prefer to scavenge among lower-class urban dustbins than risk life in the wild.

Despite the clamour over animal rights, nobody seems to have asked the foxhounds what they think. They were, presumably, put on this Earth for a purpose and without an extremely edible fox to pursue would be deprived of a useful occupation. This would make them even more of an expensive luxury than they already are. Only the rich could afford to keep them, raising the prospect - all too familiar to the RSPCA - that many would be turned loose to fend for themselves. The spectre of unemployed foxhounds tearing themselves to pieces is one that even the editors of tabloid newspapers could probably do without. There are already enough wild beasts on Dartmoor to keep the readers happy.

Many of the mink bred in captivity for a night at the opera saw the writing on the ecological wall years ago and escaped. They now live in freedom along the riverbanks, together with other escapees, such as the coypu. For them, the feel good factor is the knowledge that they will die naturally and thwart the efforts of furriers to grow rich. But what of the feelings of the delightful young ladies who step out in the West End with their wealthy protectors? Do they wish to be politically correct and refuse the offer of a mink coat? Or do they think of their old age when they will need something to keep them warm in bed? It's bad luck for the still-captive mink that most of them think of their old age. As for snakeskin shoes and matching accessories; well, snakes are horrible, wriggly things, anyway, and fewer of them would make the world a safer place.

Out East, where rich old gentlemen have not one mistress but half a dozen, they occasionally need help to perform their duties. The tiger is thought to be most useful in this respect, as is the rhinoceros. Whenever a poacher sees a tiger with his parts intact or a rhino with an extra-large bump on his nose he thinks of all the money to be made by killing the beast. No amount of pleading by the World Wildlife Fund, which estimates there are only 3,000 tigers left in India, will persuade either the poacher or the paymaster that their activities are a threat to the entire eco-system. So long as there are more wealthy Chinese than there are cures for impotence the tiger will remain an endangered species.

The exponents of political correctness have, however, made their presence felt on supermarket shelves throughout the land. To choose a box of eggs marked 'free range' - even though they are twice the price of inferior varieties produced by hens in battery cages - to proclaim your compassion to all and sundry. Only the poor and those immune to salmonella go for battery eggs. To buy free-range eggs direct from the farm smacks of penny-pinching and is not favoured by the middle-classes who much prefer to shop at Sainsburys. Not that farmers allow customers anywhere near the production line. If they did, buyers might discover that the term 'free range' was open to very liberal interpretation. In a true free-range environment, chickens would roam the countryside, pecking at worms and all sorts of nourishing grubs, and lay their eggs in the hedgerows. An urchin from the village would then have to collect them, hoping to find them before they started to hatch. In current jargon, free range means simply that chickens are not subject to leg-irons.

The same applies to little piggies which can be turned into bacon in six months or so by confining them to pens and force-feeding them in a manner once reserved for IRA prisoners. But while IRA men and women are now allowed to die of starvation, if they so wish, the piggies - which represent profit, not politics - are kept alive. The more food that can be shoved down their throats and the less room they have in which to turn round, the quicker the profit can be realised. And profit is what farming is all about.

Nobody really cares about pigs which, after all, tried to lord it over all the other animals on the farm. But calves, with or without BSE, are another matter, especially when sent abroad for making Vienna schnitzel. Like pigs, veal calves spend their short and unhappy lives in crates, waiting for the chop. The problem confronting farmers is: what else can be done with them? Their arrival in the world stems from the need to keep their mothers in lactation. But, as nature decrees that half the progeny born to dairy cattle are not equipped to produce pintas themselves, there is an inevitable surplus of male calves. The obvious way to overcome the problem is to eat them.

Unsurprisingly, the trade in veal had been going on for centuries before a lot of sentimental women and people with nothing to do discovered that the poor wee beasties were being fed an iron-free diet to keep their flesh nice and white before being schnitzelfied. As usual, the frogs are the worst offenders, closely followed in the public's estimation by farmers and hauliers. So while it is politically correct to buy free-range eggs off the supermarket shelves, it is absolutely essential to leave veal in the cold cabinet. Before p.c. became the clichè of the day, this tactic was known as a consumer boycott.

The dilemma for those who like a schnitzel before going to the bullfight wearing a mink coat is how to enjoy their lifestyle without being cruel or inhumane. The moral argument is well understood by the guardians of animal rights, such as the RSPCA, who do not hesitate to cash in on it. Every year, millions of pounds are bequeathed to charity by people with a vaguely guilty conscience - as well as by old ladies with nobody else to love. Cats and dogs are sure to loosen the purse strings, as are the unwilling occupants of scientific laboratories. The British Union for the Abolition of Vivisection spends some of the money it receives in legacies on well-publicised battles with the cosmetic companies which, it claims, carry out needless experiments. Should, for instance, shampoo be tested by dropping it into the eyes of innocent bunnies? The BUAV thinks not and the message is now getting through. Indeed, some companies have learned that the politically correct route to higher sales is by not testing their products on animals. But few people yet go to the extent of Tolstoy who once tied a chicken to the leg of a chair and said to a guest: "It you want it, you kill it." The guest ate muesli with the rest of the family.

The World Wildlife Fund, which fights a running battle with poachers in Asia and Africa, knows how easy it is to be politically incorrect. The decline of the elephant has as much to do with corruption as with the lack of a coherent conservation programme. But religion can have an equally adverse effect on animal husbandry. In India, the best way to be politically incorrect is to suggest that beef curry would make a nice change. Many of the 200 million sacred cows wandering about are in their late twenties - an age which in Europe would have consigned them at least to an own-brand tin of steak and kidney. In Argentina, they would have succumbed to foot-and-mouth long before their teens and in the United States to the relentless pursuit of profit by the Chicago meat barons. Agronomists at the World Bank have long prayed for an outbreak of anthrax to deplete the stock of economically-useless cattle. But so far the temple bells have kept the evil spirits at bay.

The Hindus are not, of course, Jews or Moslems and, if they have to kill animals, do so in a politically acceptable way. Except when engaged in conflict, they are a mild and gentle people, not given to cutting throats. The Jews and Moslems, on the other hand, happily engage in ritual slaughter every day. They will cut the throats of anything, except little piggies which both have rejected on the grounds that pork goes off rather quickly in the heat. That still leaves plenty of animal's to be separated from their souls in a ritually-correct way. For some reason, probably because there are more Jews writing for Western newspapers than Arabs, the Jewish method is ... well, kosher. But to slit an animal's throat and let the blood run down the gutter, as happens in Arab countries, is one of the more disgusting habits of the children of Allah. Why could not they collect the blood - as happens in Britain - and export it to feed hungry chickens in France?

The ultimate in ritual slaughter was, in fact, demonstrated by Britain, France and Germany in the trenches of the Somme during the first world war. Thousands of men and horses were sacrificed - and there was not a mad cow in sight.

10

Laughing all the way

Not all little piggies have their snouts chained to a trough in a steel cage. Some live in palatial surroundings, dining on pate de foie while awaiting the next share option. One, named Cedric, was taken to the annual meeting of British Gas. Next day, his picture appeared in all the newspapers. Some people thought he looked more like a fat cat. It was pure coincidence that the chief executive of British Gas, Cedric Brown, was due to address shareholders and explain how he went to market and came away vastly enriched. Mr Brown, a former gas fitter, may or may not be steeped in Orwellian culture. But he has certainly proved that, in the workplace, some little piggies are more equal than others. He has now retired from British Gas on a pension of £247,000 a year; except that until recently, he still worked for the company as a consultant on an annual fee of £120,000. Some of his former colleagues are not so lucky. They have been made redundant in the ever-widening search for economies.

Cedric Brown is, alas, not the only former State employee who was in the right place at the right time. The chairman, chief executives and plain, ordinary (some of them very ordinary) directors of privatised utilities have all shown that Victorian values are alive and well and living not far from the City of London. Even the shareholders of the new companies - pension funds, insurance companies and the like - have done little to stamp out greed. Had they been so inclined, they could easily have overturned the share option schemes designed to enrich directors, if not the public. When British Gas was floated on the Stock Exchange in 1986, it had 4.4 million shareholders who owned 62 per cent of the capital. Many of them were first-time buyers - the 'Sids' of the marketing campaign - who may not have known how to throw their weight around. It's now too late: most of Sid's shares have been bought up by the institutions which now own 85 per cent of the company. Despite a feeble hint by the Prime Minister that it was up to 'shareholders' to prevent abuses, the men in grey suits are quite happy to nod through salary increases and executive share schemes. To add insult to injury, the remaining Sids have been told they're not wanted. It is, apparently, 'inappropriate' for the company to maintain a register with 1.8 million names on it. So much for the concept of Sid-ism promoted by Margaret Thatcher. As for the thousands of British Gas workers made redundant and who now rely on State benefits, the taxpayer will pick up the bill.

Nor can the long-suffering taxpayer expect much sympathy from the merchant banks, stockbrokers and consultants of all kinds who help to bring little piggies to market. They themselves have been enriched to the tune of many millions of pounds by the privatisation programme, putting them firmly in the fat-cat category. The fees for the flotation of British Rail alone amounted to £450 million, enough to put right more than a few of the discomforts endured by commuters for many years. But in the City it does not do to be offended by greed. One never knows whose back one may have to scratch on the morrow.

The well-scratched directors of privatised companies unfortunately have some politically correct statistics to support them. Since British Telecom was privatised in 1984, millions of people have bought shares in the former public utilities. In the mid-eighties, when Sids were coming out of the woodwork in droves, there were no fewer than 12 million shareholders in the United Kingdom. This was six times as many as there had been at the end of the war. Where had they all come from? Had the British at last been persuaded of the benefits of a share-owning democracy? Or did they simply see the chance to make a quick buck as a cash-strapped government sold off the family silver? The answer is - both, even though most of them had not the faintest idea of how the Stock Exchange worked. Nor had they any conception of the risk involved. But, in an enterprise culture, to suggest that the sale of taxpayers' assets was in anything less than the national interest was most definitely p.i. The Chancellor of the Exchequer, who pocketed the proceeds, was only too happy to confirm that it was the correct political course.

In the recession-hit nineties, privatisation has lost much of its sheen, thanks largely to Cedric and his friends in the water industry. The privatisation of that particular industry, by the way, provides a superb example of ministerial double-speak. The straight-talking Michael Howard, then Secretary of State for the Environment and in charge of water privatisation, described the flotation as a great success. Nearly two million people, he said, had applied for shares in the water companies. Mr Howard is, of course, always correct, politically and in every other way. But, on the mathematical front, his description might just be open to question. The day before privatisation the companies were largely owned by the taxpayer and their dependants - all 55 million of them. Yet, by reducing the figure to nearly two million, Mr Howard was able to claim 'a great success'.

The disbenefits of privatisation have, alas, become all too clear. Prices have gone up, standards of service have gone down. Thousands of workers in the gas, water, electricity and telephone industries have lost their jobs. The sale of the family silver has turned out largely to be an exercise for the enrichment of shareholders and directors. Assets bought with taxpayers' money have in some cases been sold at a huge profit - to the new owners - to companies in the United States and France. Even the institutional shareholders so used to sitting on their hands at the annual meeting have begun to shift uncomfortably. One or two have even suggested - sotto voce, of course - that perhaps directors ought to face some sort of test before being allowed a place at the trough. But they have not quite managed to put their votes where their innermost thoughts are.

Directors such as Cedric Brown say they are worth every

penny of their salary. Perhaps they are. Perhaps their salaries are only comparable to those elsewhere in the international jobs market. If that is the case, there is a very easy and politically correct way to put their claims to the test. Let them resign and find a job at the same pay level elsewhere. That would scotch the somewhat unkind suggestion that they were fat cats who just happened to be in the right place at the right time.

A Brief Resume

Congratulations! You have survived ten chapters without succumbing to a fit of political correctness and ripping the book apart! You are clearly equipped to proceed to the second, more intellectual section. (Apologies to Cedric for consigning him to the first part.) Before moving on, however, here is a little test to see how you really shape up in the provincial world of political conformity.

Do you adjust your metaphors to suit the company or say what you mean and stick to your principles? Do you pretend to be clever, coming out (okay, you know what we mean) with verbal contortions that would make an onomasiologist blush? Do you ever wish that you had a fur coat or that the lower classes would leave their Sierras at home? Do you understand what is meant by a stakeholder society, as propounded by Tony Blair? If so, please drop the publisher a line, explaining how it differs from the old-fashioned capitalism favoured by Margaret Thatcher.

Under the citizen's charter, all taxpayers - including members of the Royal Family and the Church of England - have the right to graduate in political correctness. To qualify, just answer at least four of the following six questions. (Lesbians need attempt only three.)

1. Imagine, for a moment, that you are a product of the state education system. (You are? Ten bonus points immediately.) A friend suggests that, to avoid unemployment, you should obtain a degree in English literature. If invited to open the tomb of Shakespeare, what should you look for? Say how Shakespeare differs from Byron.

2. You have just escaped from negative equity and your home is worth £3.02 (seasonally adjusted) more than you paid for it. Do you pray for double-digit inflation

or stick to your (socialist) principles and hope that the boom will not get out of hand? Please explain whether your answer implies political correctness or political expediency.

3. How do you define racial prejudice? Would you prefer to remain homeless rather than share a squat with somebody whose skin was a different colour? Say how reggae music differs from Beethoven.

4. At a dinner party, you are placed next to a member of the opposite sex who is obviously queer. Do you 1) ask to be moved; 2) chat him or her up; 3) try to sell him/her an insurance policy while drawing a discreet veil over the need for an HIV test. If (1), calculate the odds of being placed next to another queer on the other side of the table.

5. You are invited to the funeral of Diana, Princess of Wales. Do you weep tears of joy or suspect the presence of paparazzi and put on a show of grief? Say how the speed limit in central Paris compares with that of Calcutta. What would you do with a dead Moslem and a bent Mercedes?

6. Explain how the Japanese have overcome the problem of a statutory minimum wage. Answers should be sent on a postcard to: The Chairman, Conservative and Unionist Association, Smith Square, London SW1P 3HH, marked 'LYB'.

11

Brothers in Law

Poor old Walter Raleigh! If he hadn't lost his head, a lot of opprobrium could have been heaped upon it.

First of all, there are all those fag ends. They have to be collected and disposed in a non user-friendly way by a hygiene maintenance operative in a council truck. In the old days, a tramp could be employed to patrol the streets with one foot in the gutter and a sharp eye on the lookout for free roll-your-own material. Despite the emphasis on recycling, tramps are no longer encouraged. To be down and out while at the same time ruining your health with free tobacco is politically incorrect. Then there are all those potato peelings, many of which turn green when exposed to light. Green, as explained in a previous chapter, ought to be good for you. But not in potatoes. The green bits can poison you, if the tobacco hasn't put you on death row already.

Both tobacco and potatoes, along with tomatoes, dahlias and cocaine, come from the New World, home of the American lawyer. He often works hand in glove with the American doctor. Both can - for a small fee - protect your civil rights, remove your appendix, sue the hospital for negligence and help each other to buy a new Lincoln or Cadillac every 12 months. While doctors eschew tobacco, many lawyers chew cocaine, plant dahlias and eat tomatoes (being careful to cut out the green bits, which can poison you). Of the two, it is hard to say which is the richer or more politically correct. Doctors are, however, more popular; just.

Lawyers pick up the pieces where their professional colleagues, the doctors, leave off. They can argue, for instance, that the tobacco company which supplied Elmer with two million cigarettes during the course of his life was not only irresponsible, unethical, repacious and immoral but motivated only by greed and profit - in fact, very much the same qualities that keep the American lawyer in Cadillacs. If Elmer's widow happens to be a pretty young thing who could make use of two or three million dollars, the lawyer will try even harder to win compensation. Great play will be made of the fact that Elmer was a hopeless hillbilly who couldn't read the warning labels on cigarette packets. Why, poor Elmer didn't even know what lung cancer was! This opens the door to further litigation. With the lawyer's help, Elmer's widow could sue the education authorities for allowing him to leave school in such a vulnerable condition.

Lung cancer has to be treated by the medical profession. Here a distinction has to be made immediately between American doctors, who regard medicine as a business, and British doctors, who have been told by the government to regard medicine as a business. It is, of course, politically correct to insist that under the NHS all patients have the right to free treatment at the time of need. In America, as is well known, one can die on the street unless one has the right insurance. If you're lucky, you might be picked up by the fire brigade and taken to hospital. But don't call an ambulance unless you have 500 dollars in your pocket. If by chance the fire engine runs over your foot, you should certainly call a lawyer. In fact, one may well be following the fire engine. But, on the whole, both medicine and the law are far more profitable when the patient is confined to bed.

To suggest that lung cancer is a self-inflicted wound that should not be treated at the taxpayer's expense sparks off exactly the sort of debate that lawyers love. It gives them the chance to show off their skills and demonstrate that, in a caring, compassionate society, such views are reactionary and politically incorrect. On the other hand, if their client is a hard-up, Tory-controlled health authority, they can argue the exact opposite. Sometimes a lobbyist for the tobacco companies will confuse the issue by talking about civil liberties and the right to smoke. Then somebody from ASH will come along and ask whose liberty we're talking about. Should, for instance, innocent parties, i.e., non-smokers, have to inhale secondhand smoke while eating organically-grown lobster in the most expensive restaurant in town? In America, most restaurant owners are now so terrified of the law that smokers are not allowed through the door. How Churchill would have got on had he turned up at Rules dangling that litigious wad of p.i. Havana weed from his lips is anyone's guess. Britain would almost certainly not have won the war.

Tobacco gives rise to more hot air than all the other health issues put together. Is it politically acceptable, for instance, to advertise cigarettes on television? Clearly, it is not. Yet cigarettes are advertised in newspapers and on racing cars which, like passive smoking, convey the message secondhand to those merely hoping to see somebody killed on the track. The danger is that those prevented from catching lung cancer will complain that their rights have been infringed. Smoking is not - yet - a crime and they should be allowed to get on with it. To judge by the number of people, especially young women, who persist in smoking, the health lobby has some way to go in getting its message across.

And what of the man who was given three months to live and survived for three years? Was not the medical profession grossly negligent in allowing him to exceed his allotted span? He should have joined the seals and mad cows long ago instead of being treated free of charge by the National Health Service. Had he been Chinese, the release of his soul could have been arranged at virtually no cost to the state. The Chinese believe in 'tranquil death' but sometimes they just lay people out in the square and let politics take its course. In Darwin, the erstwhile death capital of Australia, he could have been put out of his misery by a cheap and easily-administered injection. Until the Federal government put an end to the practice, a doctor would have provided the necessary documentation.

The fear of being sued by ungrateful patients is one reason why doctors have become so politically correct in recent years. They do not say 'You are a silly fool, you should have been aware of the risk and you cannot expect the state to bale you out'. Instead, they have to commiserate with the victim, promise him a bed and an operation within a prescribed period and do everything to keep him out of the hands of the undertakers. (Compare this procedure to the fate of a financial adviser who does not warn his client of the risk!) As for throwing bodies in a heap while waiting for the oven to get warm, that is fraught with danger. Exposing the corpse to ignominy can leave the mortuary open to damages. (The politically-incorrect Serbs simply dig a hole, invite the corpses-to-be to stand on the edge and cover them up. This can, however, lead to legal action in The Hague.)

But what of those who lead blameless lives, breathing the fresh dust of the asbestos factory and sprouting nothing more malignant than a pony tail? Pony tails are all right on ponies and empathically correct for the young ladies who ride them. But on men they are a sign of incipient revolt and, probably, sexual deviation. Like the flowers worn in the hair of the beautiful people during the sixties, they indicate a certain disregard for the conventions of life and seriously undermine an individual's ability to do his job. How can a man with long hair be expected to preach the gospel or sell the Encyclopaedia Britannica? But to discriminate against a person simply because he has long hair is a risky business. Discrimination is politically incorrect and can lead to damages on the sexual, racial, social, employment and just about every other front except the national. To discriminate against the National Front is perfectly all right, except in France where they collect a large number of votes.

The law is a weighty business and cannot be left simply to barristers and solicitors. In libel cases, juries have to be brought in to ensure that both sides have something worth fighting for. A million pounds could be at stake over the interpretation of the words 'She was all tit and no bum'. To help the jurors reach the correct decision and award the appropriate level of damages, judges have to be employed. Some judges are very old and have been dispensing justice for so long that they can do it with their eyes shut. If the transcript shows that the judge may well have been in this transcendental state while summing up, the astute lawyer will seize on the chance for a retrial. This will provide more work for both lawyers and judges.

Judges are the last bastion of tradition and fairness in the British Isles. They will have no truck with politics, unless they are hoping to become Lord Chancellor, and often go out of their way to assert their independence. They have the law to uphold and do so to the letter. They do not like trendy theories or politically-correct language. To them, a spade is a spade, not an implement to help the under-privileged provide themselves with the ingredients for a balanced diet. As for the unmarried woman who shares the bed of a witness, she is not a partner but a mistress, dammit! "I will not have that sort of language in my court!" exclaimed one upholder of the spade culture.

On the whole, judges are exposed to all sorts of language and cope with it very well. Some is abstruse and comes from the law books, some of which may not have been opened for many years. Some is of the four-letter variety, to be found in *Lady Chatterley's Lover* and *Last Exit to Brooklyn*. But unless they contain libel books don't come before the courts any more. This is largely because the upper classes have stopped worrying about what their servants might read. Even so, there is a vast range of legislation, couched in politically correct terms, with which judges have to grapple. In recent years, a dreadful new threat - manifesting itself in several languages - has appeared on the horizon. This is the European court; several courts, in fact, dealing with everything from premature senile dementia to the precise definition of tit and bum. Euro courts often give rise to an irrational phobia on the part of defendants who claim they are politically incorrect. Worst of all, from the British point of view, is that they are staffed entirely by foreigners wearing funny hats. In British courts, a funny hat is called a wig and is no laughing matter.

If senile dementia is determined by law, rather than by medicine, how do the courts approach the other great issues of the age, such as abortion and assisted death? Twenty years ago, it was fairly easy to say whether a person was dead or not. If the heart had stopped and the lungs no longer drew breath, that person was dead. But what if the body was attached to a life-support machine? And what if the poor departed soul had never had the chance to enjoy life? What if it had been ejected from the womb to provide a front-page story for a Sunday newspaper? The recent furore over selective abortion - in which one foetus is killed and another allowed to live - has put the issue firmly back on the political agenda. Even now, pro-life groups are scrutinising the 1967 Abortion Act as it has not been scrutinised for years. The conditions under which abortions are permitted have, to put it mildly, long been contentious. But the idea of killing one half of a pair of twins has proved to be morally repugnant. Doctors have some explaining to do if they are to remain exempt from the charge of murder.

While abortion is the current hot potato, the long-forgotten science of eugenics also surfaces from time to time to separate the politically correct from the incorrect. The late Lord Joseph, who thought of Thatcherism before the Blessed Margaret, had some interesting views on eugenics. He thought, and said so publicly, that the lower classes ought to be discouraged from breeding. This would reduce the budget for social services and have beneficial effects all round. The noble lord may well have had a valid point. Without vast numbers of lower-class brats to feed, house and educate, the upper classes - to which Lord Joseph belonged - could enjoy lower taxes and an environment free of the distressing reminders of the human condition. The problem, of course, is to define 'lower classes'. Are they ABC1s who have fallen on hard times, possibly as a result of Thatcherite economics, or are they our coloured brethren from the inner cities, natural supporters of the Labour Party? In any case, the lower classes, of whatever colour, could hardly be trusted to vote Tory. So castrating them or forcing the Pill down their gullets was as good a way as any to reduce the Labour vote.

Economically and socially, it may have been a good idea, favoured by the managers of the National Health Service who could devote their resources to deserving members of the upper classes. But at the time it was deemed to be politically incorrect. Eugenics was the sort of thing promoted by Herr Hitler in his efforts to produce a super race. Sir Keith, a Jew, could never support that. He was simply thinking of the PSBR. But the episode did him little harm. He was made a peer of the realm and described as the intellectual bastion of the Conservative Party (or the Mad Monk, depending on the circumstances). The Iron Lady herself had a few kind words to say on his death. As far is known, his death was entirely natural and not assisted in any way.

The debate has now moved on and centres on the disbenefits to the state of people living too long. Death is the great liberator - of souls and of the assets of those who no longer have a use for them. The Dutch have managed to overcome both the legal and ethical objections to euthanasia and allow doctors to kill people. It would be helpful if the old folk could be persuaded to kill themselves. But some are so confused by the ravages of pre-senile dementia that they can't remember where they put the tablets, let alone the share certificates. Very few are able, like Arthur Koestler and his wife, to face up to life and commit suicide.

Ironically, doctors themselves are among the high-risk category when it comes to ending it all. They see so much death that life becomes unbearable. If only lawyers would suffer the same pangs of conscience.

11 (refresher)

The Wronged Fare Well

She was in a bad way. Her eyes had a haunted look and the mink was way past its wear-by date. Her hands trembled as she fumbled for a cigarette.

"Allow me," I said, reaching across the desk and offering her a light.

"Thanks," she murmured, drawing nervously on the weed and exhaling a cloud of smoke. I preferred her perfume, which suggested hazards of a financial kind.

"So, you're Marlowe," she purred, surveying me through lashes so long they just had to be false.

"At your service, ma'am."

I wondered how she was going to pay for that service. I was running a business, not a charity for hard-up bimbos.

"I need some money, Marlowe," she confided, just in case the smoke had impaired my vision. "I'm going back to school."

"Forgive me, Miss..er..?"

"Kazinski."

"Forgive me, Miss Kazinski, but aren't you a little ... mature ... for elementary biology?"

"Don't get me wrong, Marlowe. I'm not going to put on a gymslip. I'm speaking metaphorically."

The mink might have been mangy but the dame had class. You don't get many metaphors in my trade; just split infinitives.

"Sorry, ma'am. I don't follow."

She crossed her legs, then uncrossed them again and blew more nicotine my way. There was a word for this type of dame. It wasn't nice.

"You see, Marlowe, I failed at school because I was bullied. Harassed psychologically and physically."

"And you lost your virginity behind the bicycle shed?"

"You still wearing your own teeth, Marlowe?"

"Yes, ma'am."

"Then you've been extremely lucky, my friend."

The dame didn't look like she could damage my molars but I was taking no chances. I rolled with the punch, metaphorically speaking.

"I just wanted to establish the facts," I replied.

"You can leave that to my lawyer."

"Lawyer, eh?"

The plot was beginning to thicken. It always did when the law was involved. I wondered if she was on legal aid.

She opened her bag - crocodile, with a hint of moonlight - and pulled out a flask. Pouring herself a slug of neat liquor, she downed it in one gulp and walked to the window.

"You see? I can't even walk straight. That's because I failed my O-level German."

"Lay off the bottle and you could pass A-level Esperanto," I said. "You could even conduct your own case."

She sat down again, stubbed out the cigarette in my coffee cup and recrossed her legs. They were nice legs, as far as I could see, which was far enough.

"The fact is, Marlowe, I'm suffering from post traumatic stress disorder. My entire life has been blighted by what happened at school. The bicycle shed was just the start."

"So?"

"I'm planning to sue for damages."

"And where do I come in?"

"You collect the evidence."

I had to think fast. The dame might have been classy but she was no chicken. I didn't fancy digging up evidence that was twenty years old or more.

"I'm a private dick, not an archaeologist," I said.

"What's that supposed to mean?"

"It could be a time-consuming job. In my profession, time is money."

She pinned me to the chair with eyes that were as hard as diamonds, but without the sparkle. I had a feeling it was my turn to develop a haunted look.

"What makes you think you're so different to anybody else?" she asked.

It was rhetorical question to which there was no answer. I waited for the dame to continue.

"This shyster of a lawyer has offered me a deal," she said. "No win, no fee."

"That's not how I work."

"He reckons that if we can stitch up the governors we can screw them for a hundred grand. Split four ways," she added.

Even I didn't need O-level maths for that. The dame was becoming interesting.

"And I get twenty five per cent. Right?"

"Wrong. Twenty."

"Hell, I do all the work and get the smallest cut!" I protested.

"And who does all the suffering? You and that schmuck of a lawyer are just coming along for the ride."

"All the same, Miss Kazinski, I rather think..."

She cut me dead with a look that could only have been picked up on the country-house circuit at about 3 am. She stood up.

"Goodbye, Marlowe. I guess my legal adviser was right. You're a jerk."

She started towards the door. Her progress was steady and revealed no sign of either stress or liquor. I figured that twenty per cent was better than nothing.

"Now, wait a minute," I said, swallowing hard. "Let's not be hasty. Like I said, I'm a pro. I'll dig."

A smile hovered about her lips as she removed her hand slowly from the door. I indicated the chair on the client side of the desk.

"I just thought it might be better to consult a doctor first," I said weakly.

"The law comes first," she said, sitting down. "We can always buy a medical opinion later."

The dame wasn't so dumb, after all. I wondered if she had a degree in economics.

"And he gets twenty per cent, too?" I asked.

"That's none of your business."

"I believe in equality. What about your counsellor?"

"The last one got a kick in the balls. He thought that stroking my thigh was part of the treatment."

She lit another cigarette and directed a lethal dose of carcinogens towards me. I was living dangerously in this dame's company.

"You're not a lesbian, by any chance, Miss Kazinski?"

"Lutheran," she replied.

"Pity you're not Jewish. You could have upped the ante for racial discrimination."

"You keep your hands to yourself, Marlowe, and I might up your ante."

"It's a deal. Where do I start looking?"

"Buy yourself a one-way ticket to Cheltenham and make a few enquiries," she said. "Maybe put an ad in the paper."

"What about expenses? I like to eat."

She took a crumpled £50 note from her bag and, with barely a second glance, pushed it across the desk.

"That should cover the fare as well, luvvy."

"Thanks," I said, wondering how the dame herself was going to eat that night. But anybody with a mink coat and a taste for nicotine had to be a survivor.

"Goodbye," she said, extending her hand. "And take care. I don't want you stressed out before the case gets to court."

"There's a lot of it about," I said. "You'd better give me the name of your lawyer."

But the dame had already gone. I opened the window to clear the smog and wondered how I would cope if I ever went down with pre-senile dementia.

12

Chairpersons, Inc

It is no coincidence that the Monster Raving Loony Party had its first taste of electoral success in local government. Town halls up and down the land are full of loonies, some Left, some Right, some a rainbow mixture of democratic delusions. They all have one thing in common: a pathological desire to be politically correct and pave the way to the great asylum on the Thames, the Palace of Westminster.

For many years, before the Euro-sceptic wing of the Conservative Party came along, the sole right to be politically correct was in the hands of the Labour Party. Nothing that could possibly be explained in simple, straightforward English was allowed to escape the corrective process. The gender benders, the rampant lesbians, the deaf, dumb and otherwise disabled members of the Gay Wheelwrights' Community Workshop all had their moment of glory. The lexicographers of the loony Left were in their element, replacing worn-out verbs with trendy new nouns. To be addressed as 'chairman' when you were clearly (well, perhaps not all that clearly) a woman was the ultimate insult. It's just as well that only 30 per cent of voters bother to turn out for local government elections. Any more and the loonies would be able to claim that people took them seriously.

In those far-off days when Conservatives controlled a large number of local authorities in Britain, the loony ones could be clearly identified. The Greater London Council, a huge regional asylum separated from Westminster by a river, was in the grip of a terrible man, Red Ken, who kept newts in the bath. The iron maiden who in all things was the epitome of political correctness decided that newts were not an acceptable hobby for a man with ambitions to cross the river. She therefore neutered the GLC by selling its goods and chattels to the Japanese who wanted to open a shushi bar. (On a foggy night in London town, it is very hard to tell the difference between raw fish and a newt sandwich.)

In time, the iron lady herself became the meat in the sandwich and was invited to conduct a tour of the Channel Tunnel, then in the process of being electrified. The man in grey who replaced her soon managed to purge the country of Right-wing nonsense by losing virtually every seat held by the Tories in local government. This, the spin doctors explained, was merely a ploy to make the real loonies - in the Liberal and Labour parties - stand out more. It also enabled voters to make an informed, rational choice. This was important in a democracy, even one without a strategic authority for its largest city.

For some reason, probably the high level of air pollution, inner-city councils tend to be more loony than those in the shires. A daily diet of lead and carbon monoxide can undoubtedly affect the mind, even more so than roast beef. We are, after all, what we breathe. In heavily-congested zones, such as Liverpool, Newcastle and Birmingham, the proportion of monster ravers during the sixties and seventies sparked off the well-founded belief that a loonier-than-thou policy was in force throughout the entire country. In retrospect, the occasional outbreak of loonyism in the shires was perhaps an early sign - alas, undetected - that BSE was already in the food chain.

To be a member of a large council, perhaps even the chairperson, was certainly a way to make a name for oneself. Some councillors, like Dame Shirley Porter, the former Miss Cohen, already had a name: even among enemies it was usually unprintable. Others, like T. Dan Smith, the leader of Newcastle-upon-Tyne council, had to acquire one through sheer hard work. He was not a Tesco heiress but merely the PR man for an architect named Poulson. Sometimes councillors moved heaven and earth to further the dictates of central government. Thus it came to be that a vast swathe of Porterland - otherwise known as the

City of Westminster - was cleared of drunks and deadbeats and sold to yuppies who, on balance, were thought more likely to vote Conservative. As for all those dead socialists in the graveyard, they could be farmed out to private enterprise. In the hot-house atmosphere of the politically-acquiescent eighties, this was perceived to be the way forward. In the cooler nineties, the policy of selling council houses has been shown to have had fault lines.

As Red Ken proved, local government can be a thorn in the flesh of Her Majesty's ministers. A lot of money is involved, a fact which had not escaped the notice of John Poulson and many others. The men at Westminster, when not busy tabling questions of their own, like to know how that money is spent. Some of it, they suspect, is wasted on bread-and-breakfast accommodation for foreigners and workshare projects for the unemployed. In fact, most is spent on education which offers tremendous scope for instilling politically-correct thoughts in little minds, often in a multi-ethnic environment. "Kwame might have a funny name, Frankie, but he is no different to the rest of us, despite what your old grandfather says." In counties where 95 per cent of the children are white, the little Kwames can be absorbed with a patronising display of political correctness. As the proportion of Little Black Sambos increases and that of white, Anglo-Saxon protestants declines, the quality of mercy becomes somewhat strained. (The exception is Northern Ireland where the quality of mercy is seldom extended to either Catholics or Protestants, even if they are white.) By the time political correctness has reached the inner cities, the whole ethos of local government has changed. In Birmingham and Bradford, exam results have to be interpreted non-racially, playing down the ability of Asian children to obtain the most A-levels. But to draw a distinction between Asians and Afro-Caribbeans is politically incorrect. Are not negroes as clever as Pakistanis? Of course they are, as are the Arabs who fill private crammers up and down the country.

The Tories, ever far-sighted, spotted the dangers of

politically-correct school teachers and education committees early on. To purify the system, they sacked the teachers and put education in the hands of those, such as master butchers, who knew a thing or two about syntax and irregular verbs. After all, the wrong sort of education, particularly that provided at the taxpayer's expense, would only store up trouble for the future. Old Inner Citeans might turn out to be the sort of people who kept newts in the bath or demanded cheap fares on the Underground just as it was about to be privatised. Old Etonians, on the other hand, were familiar with the ways of the world and could always be touched for a few quid at election times. (At other times, it was best to approach them with a whip before making contact.)

Political correctness is, of course, the prerogative of those elected to serve on local authorities and pursue the party line. The employees of such concerns are condemned by law to be political eunuchs, trapped between the loonies in the council chamber and the lesbians of the Rainbow Loop Alliance (the loopies). They are forced to take an impartial view, balancing the needs of the loopies against the power of the loonies, whether it leads to ulcers or not. Sometimes they have to seek the protection of the law to keep the loopies out of the council chamber and the loonies out of their hair. It's hardly surprising that, after a hard day serving the public, some employees are not as impartial as they should be. Some, in fact, are unable to distinguish between an newt-waving loony and a self-employed plumber who needs a roof over his head.

Some councils actually still maintain one or two safe houses for the poor and needy, despite being told to make over their stock to the housing associations. Sometimes the safe houses are occupied not by the poor and needy but by friends and relatives of council employees. That, of course, is perfectly legitimate. Such people have to live somewhere. And, as the Rowntree Foundation observed in a recent report, the trend towards home-ownership in Britain has probably gone too far. Not everybody wants to help the building societies become banks so that they can evict defaulters without feeling bad about it. There is no stigma attached to living in a council house, especially at election times. If there were, the Tories would have put out a poster about it.

It is on council estates that political hopefuls on the local scene often have the advantage over aspirants to Westminster. Many actually live there and are familiar with the prejudices of the drug pushers and wife beaters whose votes the solicit. Most Members of Parliament of the raving Right variety have never been nearer a council estate than the Constitutional Club where they dispense advice over a gin and tonic. The foot-sloggers who knock at the doors are party hacks who, in due course, will get a letter of thanks from the successful/unsuccessful candidate.

To knock at a strange door, however, is fraught with ideological pitfalls. The enemy within could demand your views on public lavatories for the genderly bent (loopy loos) or an end to the malicious gossip about the Rainbow Alliance (loopy lies). If the door knocker himself is inclined to rave, he will be written off as a loony and the door slammed in his face. But more often than not the householder will simply confront him with an everyday story of life on a council estate. Should, for instance, a white family with only one ghetto blaster between them be forced to live next to a black family with a taste for reggae played in the middle of the night? Should a black family, hard-working and teetotal, be subjected to the insults of drunken yobboes whose rottweilers roam the estate without a muzzle? To answer these and other questions in a politically-correct way, the candidate has occasionally to gloss over the fine print in the election manifesto.

And what of the boys in blue who are often called to sort out problems on the estate? They have to be impartial as well as legally correct, which is why so many of their reports are couched in such extraordinary language. To ensure that grammatical mistakes are kept to a minimum, the Watch Committee has installed a number of bugging devices in police stations. These can detect the most subtle nuance in discussions with the accused, such as a kick in the groin, and emit a piercing whine if any racially-offensive remarks are made. Of course, we all know that the average cop is not terribly keen on the average black, even if by some mischance he happens to be one of them. But interrogators must at all times maintain a politically-correct posture and be careful not to tread on anyone's toes, or fingers, or leave any mark that might prejudice their enquiries. Moreover, the black bastards who share the drugs trade with the Mafia can afford some very expensive lawyers, putting tremendous pressure on the police to extract a confession. Unless they can prove that the suspect injured himself while trying to escape with a sack of cocaine, the expensive lawyer can make life difficult. He can even take them to the Commission for Racial Equality or the European Court of Human Rights. In the Punjab, Turkey, Malawi or any of the Confederate states he'd be charged with wasting police time.

The boys in blue are often accused of being male chauvinist pigs. Certainly, their treatment of the girls in blue - in the back of a Panda car or in a cell unused for the night - does not always comply with the strictest standards of either the law or chivalry. Sometimes, it's alleged, they even bar the way to promotion for crime busters in skirts. On other occasions, it's alleged they do not like homosexuals. In the Royal Ulster Constabulary, even Catholics are not immune to discrimination! But until the RUC appoints a black, homosexual Catholic to guard the Reverend Ian Paisley, chief constables throughout the UK will continue to receive letters from expensive lawyers.

The public obsession with law and order obscures one of the more insidious aspects of crime prevention: the Neighbourhood Watch. The Tories are very keen on Neighbourhood Watch which helps - along with special constables - to keep down the cost of law enforcement. The Nazis operated a similar scheme in the thirties although they tended not to shout about it. The Gestapo simply sent round a man in a long, black coat to see what you were doing. In politically-correct Britain, the man in the dirty raincoat might well turn out to be Uncle Fred on a nocturnal visit to Mrs Jones. That is of no concern to anybody - except, perhaps, Mr Jones and a divorce lawyer. But Uncle Fred's movements will have been noted by the peeping toms behind their net curtains and possibly even transmitted down the hot line to the user-friendly police station. Should a garden gnome be missing in the morning, Uncle Fred will be under a cloud.

To suggest that such schemes are anti-social and pander to the prurient undermines the efforts of all Right-thinking people (and the insurance companies) to put criminals behind bars. What's wrong with being watched? The IRA might object but the burgeoning security industry, which thrives on the fear of crime, certainly wouldn't. Nor would retailers whose sole purpose in life is to sell you a burglar alarm or a video camera. To them, Big Brother means Big Business. The only jarring note is that many private security firms are run by criminals. As Juvenal asked, 'Who will guard the guards?'. Perhaps that is another job for Neighbourhood Watch or, possibly, even the police.

The problem of loonies, loopies and light-fingered ladies is not confined to Britain. Town halls from St. Louis to Ekaterinburg provide stomping grounds for all sorts of lunatics to parade their foibles and phobias. In the United States, a lawyer rather than a man in a white coat will ensure that his client is allocated ranting space at the forum. Nor are the Russians any more immune to the corrosive effects of free speech and a market economy. In Siberia today, a handful of dollars can buy an entire council, willing to sell the region's natural resources to Burundi with no questions asked. But at least the Russians have an excuse for politically-incorrect behaviour. The only way to survive in the former peoples' republic is to accept a little gratuity on the side. Under the Soviet system, only managers of State enterprises were allowed to feather their nests. Now anybody can do it. But one has to be aware of the new free-market vocabulary. The term 'comrade', which once implied eternal friendship and a share of the spoils, is now one of abuse.

Just to confuse matters, the head comrade in Britain is now a chair.

12 (supp.)

The Wind Also Rises

The wind blew up the river, from the east. It was a chill wind, straight off the North Sea. In summer, it would have been warm and full of vinegar from the whelk stalls on Southend Pier. But it wasn't summer; it was winter and the wind left in its wake only dead leaves and bits of garbage that had fallen off the barge on the way to the dumping ground beyond the estuary.

I huddled in the doorway, thinking how good it was to be out of the wind now that winter was here. I remembered the Congo where it was hot all the year round and the air was filled with the stench of rotting corpses. A lot of people died then. I didn't. I was destined to survive and grow old.

And now I was on the streets of London, alone and unwanted. I pulled the sleeping bag around my ears and hoped that stray dogs would not be out on a night like this. It was a good sleeping bag and it had been given to me by Crisis, the charity for the homeless. I tried to think what it was like to sleep in a proper bed, with blankets and sheets and perhaps a hot-water bottle so that I could take my socks off before going to sleep. But there was no hot water here; just me and my sleeping bag and the smell of old socks.

I felt in my pocket to check that the newt sandwich was still there. It was. It was a good sandwich, full of fresh newt and some ketchup I had saved from lunch at the mission. My God, I thought, this is going to be the best newt sandwich I've ever had. My stomach rumbled gently in anticipation.

I remembered my first newt. It was up in Nottingham, just after the war. There were lots of newts then, in ponds and shady ditches. My friend Gatz said they were only fish in disguise and would make a good stew. We had an old saucepan but when we put them in they climbed out again. Gatz said we should boil the water first but I said it was quicker to grill them. They were good newts in Nottingham that year and I was sorry when the builders filled in the pond and put up houses.

My fingers curled round the edge of the bread, making sure the newt was still in the middle. I didn't want newt in the sleeping bag with me, unless it was between two slices of bread. It was good bread, straight from the supermarket, and I had paid for it with good money, collected from passers-by. I wouldn't say I was a beggar; just an old soldier two newts short of a sandwich.

The wind was still blowing up the river, past the barrage and along the rows of yuppie apartments that used to be warehouses and where I worked when there was work to be done. But now there was no work and the warehouses had been turned into rabbit hutches for the rich. I wondered if the developers employed the same builders who had filled in the pond and put an end to our barbecues in Nottingham.

I looked at the clock on the church tower opposite. A quarter to one. The wind was still blowing and the lights were going out in the rabbit hutches where I used to work before they were turned into flats for the rich. But now there was no work and I was alone in the sleeping bag with a dead newt and two slices of wholesome bread from the supermarket.

I tried to sleep but sleep wouldn't come. The wind picked up a plastic bag and tossed it around until the bag escaped from the doorway and swirled onwards down the street. I wondered whether to eat my newt sandwich or save it for breakfast. I really needed to eat it now to stave off the pangs of hunger. But there's no fun in eating a newt sandwich in the dark so I put it off till morning.

Eventually sleep must have come because I awoke to find a man in a dog collar offering me a cup of tea and a boiled egg. It was the same every morning except that on some days the egg was a sausage. Sometimes it was a pie that had passed its sell-by date. But what I needed today was a cup of tea to wash down the dust of the night.

"And how are we today?" the man in the dog collar asked, offering me the sugar bowl.

"Fine, thank you, Father," I said. "I've been sorely tried by the wind, though."

"I've got some bicarb in the car," the priest replied. "That should fix it."

"No, the wind from the river," I said. "It's blowing straight from the east."

"That's not so good," he replied. "But it will stop soon, I expect."

"I hope so, Father."

He rummaged in the bag that hung from his shoulder and produced a sheet of paper.

"I've found the address you were asking for the other day," he said. "Here. This will put you on the map again."

"Thank you, Father," I said. "I'll be in touch with them as soon as I can arrange a contest."

"If you like, I'll have a word with the Press."

"That might not be such a bad idea."

I folded the sheet of paper and put it in my pocket next to the newt sandwich and took a sip of tea. It was good tea, hot and strong, and it washed away the dust of the night. With half a cupful inside of me, I was in the mood to tackle the newt sandwich.

"I'll be back in the morning," the priest said. "Take care of yourself and keep out of the wind."

"I'll try," I said. "And thank you for the address."

I arranged the sleeping bag around my shoulders and prepared to eat my breakfast. The egg was good - all of it, not just part of it. The curate knew how to cook an egg all right.

I felt in my pocket and took out the newt sandwich. It was a good sandwich, as good as any I had ever tasted. The bread was not as fresh as it had been yesterday but the flavour of the newt had improved. It reminded me of a kipper I had once had at Quaglino's. But that was a long time ago, when I was working on the waterfront, not sleeping in shop doorways.

By the time I had finished, the sun was beginning to rise over the church tower. Soon, the street would be filled with people hurrying to work. Most were too pre-occupied to notice me; others regarded me as an eyesore.

Once in a while somebody stopped to give me money and ask what I was doing there. I told them there was no work for somebody of my age and you could see the look of terror in their eyes. They knew I was speaking the truth and that, one day, they would wake up and find themselves old. Only the young ones laughed at the old soldier in his sleeping bag and scurried over the bridge to the City.

The priest who made his rounds of the homeless every day at dawn never asked questions. He just brought me tea or coffee and something to eat. I figured that one day he would try to get me across the street and into the church. But he never did. He just brought the tea and coffee and the address of the Guinness Book of Records that I had asked for.

I wondered why nobody had claimed the record for eating raw newts before. They were no worse than oysters or some of the things I saw being cooked in the Congo. Perhaps newt swallowing was not regarded as an achievement; or perhaps the RSPCA would step in to prevent it. I hoped the Press would generate enough publicity to make it a fair contest.

I felt in my pocket to make sure I had not missed any of the newt filling from the sandwich. But it had all gone. I wondered what I would have for lunch and where I would find enough newts, now that the ponds had been filled in, to make a contest possible. Perhaps somebody on the council would know.

I lay back in the sleeping bag and felt the wind coming up again. Only this time it was not from the river.

13

Steady there, Eddie

Exports, as Harold Macmillan remarked, can be fun. They give the workforce something to do and provide the salesman with an excuse for submitting his expenses in Cantonese. They can also be extremely profitable, provided the Customs officer doesn't enquire too closely about their destination. Should the words Chile, Libya or Iraq appear on the documentation, awkward questions might be asked, especially if the exquisite little salt shakers bound for the Gulf could, with a little imagination, be turned into hand grenades.

The financiers of the City of London are not too well up on geography; nor do they understand the nuts and bolts of exports. That is for industrialists and people in overalls, not pin-striped suits. The City is concerned with balance sheets and profits. If a company is doing well, the security analysts get so excited that they forget to ask where the goods are being sold. They could ask the Department of Trade but, like the Treasury computer, that might not provide the politically-correct answer. So, until informed to the contrary, they assume that all is above board and tickety-boo. Only when the chairman absconds to Cyprus or falls from his yacht off the Canaries do they cut short their lunch hour and get out the atlas. If that reveals the slightest whiff of non-conformity, they will check their personal portfolio and put in a swift order to sell.

In private, the pin-striped piranhas of the City of London couldn't give a stuff about political correctness, so long as the money is right and readily available. If it is, they will do whatever is necessary to earn a crust, whether the public approves or not. In recent years, the public has generally not approved. The constant stench of scandal over the Square Mile - from insider trading to the misuse of pension funds - has led many to think there might be something in political correctness, after all. Is it politically defensible, for instance, for the City to maintain a system of self-regulation? The late John Smith (a less-demonic version of Tony Blair) thought that self-regulation led to self-protection. He was probably right. The watchdog won't bark if it relies on the market for its bone. Not that a statutory body, such as exists in the United States, would succeed in stamping out greed and corruption. But at least it would look better.

There is already clear blue water between the Up-U's of the greed fraternity and the Non-U's of the back office. The Up-U's will sell the pound, force up interest rates, wipe billions off share prices and enjoy a bottle of champagne at the end of the day without the slightest twinge of remorse. The national interest is not their interest. The Non-U's, burdened by mortgages and the need to buy foreign currency for their annual holiday, take a more jaundiced view. Some can even see the advantages of a single currency. But they keep quiet because their salaries depend on the freedom of the Up-U's to sell the pound down the river. To rock the boat would be politically incorrect - and that is a luxury reserved for those on the trading floor.

In real terms (a favourite phrase in the City), political correctness is essentially no different to what Professor Galbraith called the conventional wisdom. The conventional economic wisdom is the curse of the age: invisible, pernicious and all-pervasive. It affects every aspect of financial policy, stultifying every decision by the Treasury and the Bank of England with a political predictability. The conventional wisdom holds, for instance, that inflation is the great danger. Why? Because it erodes the savings of old people who are more likely to vote Conservative than those hoping to pay off their mortgage the easy, inflationary way. Even more predictable is the conventional view that the best way to control inflation is by putting up interest rates. This might well be described as the homoeopathic cure: acceptable in Royal circles but economic voodoo to everybody else. But such is the pressure to conform that nobody - well, hardly anybody - dares to suggest that you don't cure inflation by putting up the price of money.

The conventional wisdom not only distorts the markets, which should be constantly exposed to contrary thought, but stifles individuality. Just look at the fate of those who do not conform. Tiny Rowland, former chief executive of Lonrho, was virtually frozen out because of his unorthodox approach. Fortunately, Tiny thrived on adversity and made himself a small fortune (estimated at £250 million) by trading with p.i. regimes from Rhodesia to Argentina. Others, higher up the social scale than a man who once carried bags at Euston Station, wear their pin-stripes and conform. They, alas, cannot afford an independent air, despite their c.v. and public-school education.

A young man whose views are constantly out of line with those of his superiors will not get far in the City of London. Only on the trading floor, where the ability to make money is the sole criterion, will the holder of non-conventional wisdom prove his worth. A really brilliant trader, such as Nick Leeson, will even impress the mandarins at the oldest and most prestigious of merchant banks. He will be given his own trading account and use of the company's yacht. Foreign exchange dealers, commodity brokers, even the humble bond salesman will be forgiven all manner of eccentricities so long as they turn in a profit. Of course, they won't be invited to play polo at the weekend because that might embarrass the host and less well-off guests. But woe betide the whizz kid whose profits turn out to be mirages. The City will appoint its own execution squad.

It will also snap shut like a clam if rumours of financial impropriety involve a member of the Establishment - that is to say, one of the people the trader didn't meet at the polo. Strangely enough, the City can put up with sexual peccadilloes so long as they don't affect the balance sheet or ruffle the carpet at the Bank of England. It is money that counts and provided the watchdog doesn't begin to twitch in his sleep life can go on as usual. But should the computer indicate the unauthorised transfer of funds to a numbered account in Liechtenstein some lunch dates might be hastily cancelled. Ernest Saunders ("I'm not a man well versed in City affairs") is not the only person to have been smitten with amnesia. Many a City type who has suddenly discovered that his closest friend is not quite kosher is unable to recall when they last shared a bottle of Chateau Rothschild.

The best place to observe political tension at work is probably the Bank of England. Despite her aspirations to be fully independent, the Old Lady still has to do as she is told. The Governor has to take great care to be politically correct, even if he is now allowed to set the level of interest rates all by himself. Until very recently, any difference of opinion between the Governor and the Chancellor - his political master at the Treasury, a mile away to the west - was kept firmly under wraps lest it upset the markets. Now - good heavens! - disagreements are aired in public and exacerbated by teenage scribblers. Some have even expressed doubts about letting the Old Lady out on her own, especially beyond the protective walls of the City.

In theory, any conflict between the Governor and the Chancellor ought to be good for the economic well-being of the nation because somewhere between the divergent views should lie the truth. But because both are tarred with the brush of conventionality few truly radical ideas emerge. Moreover, the Bank is rather too full of its own importance, fearful that any outbreak of free speech might frighten the dreadful foreigners who leave their money in Britain. The desire to appear both wise and conventional is the single most stifling influence on economic debate. Even the 'wise men' called in to advise the government invariably agree with one another; not because they wish to appear politically correct but because they themselves have fallen prey to the conventional wisdom.

In recent years, the conventional wisdom has given rise to what might be called the formula school of economics, i.e., $x + y = c$. That, of course, is not the case and never will be where money is at stake. Yet, by applying the formula to virtually any statement by the Bank or the Treasury, the hacks are able to print what will happen to share prices or the pound. This would never have happened in the days of Montague Norman, a remote and distant Governor who liked to keep the markets guessing. How very different from the thought processes of our own dear Eddie George! Mr George's views have been set in stone for the past 30 years. Everybody knows he will oppose a cut in interest rates, because he always has done. Unlike the opaque Mr Norman, Eddie is entirely transparent. Any schoolboy with a taste for formulae can see straight through him.

The Governor is nevertheless a power to be reckoned with in the City of London. He is in charge of the commercial banks - all 640 of them - and tries to ensure that they toe the line; not the political line but the law of the land. Sometimes he suffers from a peculiar blind spot - the Bank has no windows on the outside world - and fails to see that a bank has gone bust, or is going bust, or will go bust unless the Old Lady comes to the rescue. This often calls for a dynamic, unconventional approach where conformity goes out of the - window. Sometimes, as in the case of Barings, the Bank can persuade others to pick up the pieces. In others, such as the Bank of Credit and Commerce International, the responsibility can be off-loaded to a rich old sheikh in the Gulf. In any event, the politically-correct course is not to spend taxpayers' money unless absolutely essential. In this, we can rely on Mr George rather more than on his political masters in Whitehall.

Virtually all of the 600 banks under the Old Lady's control offer a safe haven to those seeking a refuge from the economic vicissitudes of life. In countries such as Iraq, customers are very often denied the choice of cheque book. This is in clear contravention of the UN Charter on Human Rights and so it behoves the banks to offer their services to anybody with a few million pounds to spare. The Bank of

England, which spends most of the day protecting the pound, cannot afford to be too fussy over this. It is far better that presidential salaries are banked in London than disappear into some anonymous vault in Zurich. As for allegations that the Mafia washes its money whiter than white with the help of British, American and Dutch banks, that is simply a foul lie put about by those who do not understand the banking system. How is a banker to know where the money comes from? Just because a nice South American gentleman arrives at the counter with a suitcase full of dollar bills or lire that does not mean he has relatives in Sicily. It's just that the banks in Medellin would be closed by the time he arrived there on the late plane.

And what of the 'hot' money that is constantly on the move in search of a more lucrative income? The transfer of such funds around the world can put a strain on the system, especially if the return in one country is totally out of line with that in another. The Bank of England does not really like flows of such volatile funds into the country - but it dislikes even more the possibility that they might flow out again. So, to keep the money here and boost the reserves, it doesn't make life too difficult for the owners of such funds. Anybody with a billion dollars to place on deposit can easily find a bank willing to accept responsibility. But if one of its backroom boys can actually prove that the money came from drugs or other illicit enterprises the Bank can freeze the funds and adopt a politically-correct stance that no amount of legal threats from the Mafia will shake.

The men from the Mafia often have a keener grasp of economics than the men from the Ministry. They take an entirely worthy and pragmatic view that money is money, no matter where it comes from or how it is spent. One of the more lunatic theories pursued by the late Conservative government in Britain was that some fivers were better than others. In Orwellian terms, private money good, public money bad. Anybody - especially Sicilian farmers who rely on European funds - could have told them that public money can be spent, taxed, put to work or even recycled as private money. The Stock Exchange even has a film, entitled the Money-go-Round, which explains the process. No, the politically-correct way to deal with the Mafia is to slash public spending.

Fortunately for the millions of unemployed who exist on state benefits, politicians have found it extremely difficult to cut public spending. The Tories, however, found it fairly easy to cut the higher-rate tax bands for the likes of Cedric Brown. The theory is that, without fiscal incentives, the fat cats would pack their bags and leave for the Galapagos Islands. It is, of course, a particularly heinous crime to point out that during the eighties, when Britain enjoyed a period of rapid growth, the top rate of income tax was 60 per cent. The so-called entrepreneurs on whom the country apparently relied didn't run off. They stayed and were stimulated to greater efforts by the need to pay their income tax.

How awful if the new Labour government broke its election pledge not to raise taxes and gave a new twist to the Up-U economy!

STOP PRESS

A doctor writes: In the early months of 1998, Mr George was clearly under the weather and on two successive occassions opposed a rise in interest rates. This, however, was probably a seasonal aberration and, before his term of office expires, the patient will have made a full recovery.

14

Too much of a good thing

And so, at last, we arrive at the final whistle-stop on the railroad to political correctness: censorship.

Virtually no country can claim to be, or have been, entirely free of restrictions on the spoken or written word. For the vast majority of people throughout the Third World, those restrictions are part of their daily lives. Even in 'progressive' countries, the censor operates with the tacit agreement of those who wish to publish but not be damned. In uncivilised backwaters, where even Enid Blyton can be a threat to the social mores, he clamps down hard. Jails from Angola to Zimbabwe are full of people rash enough to print matter inimical to the smooth running of a one-party state. Sometimes it is not the jails that are full but the graveyards.

Even in Britain, it is only a few years since the Establishment dictated what the lower orders could read or watch. The Lord Chamberlain, who was God as far the theatre was concerned, still wielded his rod as late as 1968 when the post was finally abolished. His decline was foreshadowed by the trial of Lady Chatterley, whose bucolic romps with the gamekeeper Mellors put her publishers in the dock. When they skipped free, other publishes rushed to bring out books reflecting the 'language of real life'. They have been able to print such garbage without fear of prosecution ever since. It would be wrong, however, to think that censorship no longer exists in Britain. The editors of Right-wing newspapers can be relied upon to sweep all but the worst excesses of Conservative politicians under the carpet. And, until there is a Freedom of Information Act, the government itself can censor anything of importance - such as how Berkshire came to be radioactive.

The censor has a long and mainly dishonourable history. The Romans were the first to recognise that information is power - and they had no wish to let power slip from their own hands. In Russia, the tsars had it down to a fine art. Nothing got past the censor, especially under Nicholas I, and anybody who tried to undermine his authority with subversive ideas was not given a second chance. Dostoyevsky was among the few who survived the firing squad and learned to write in the prison camps of Siberia. He also, alas, learned to crawl there.

When the revolution finally overthrew the Tsar, the censor was among those granted a reprieve. Indeed, under the Communists he flourished as never before. If they wished to eat, literary comrades had to toe the line. Books, films, plays, even music, had to be politically correct. Anything that did not please the Kremlin was shredded, along with its creator. The successes were hailed over the airwaves of Radio Moscow as the triumph of socialism. The Americans responded with their own propaganda, letting the CIA educate the Russians via Radio Free Europe. Even the British did their bit. The Foreign Office thought that Orwell's *Animal Farm* might upset the Russians and urged that it was not published. Fortunately, commercial instincts won the day - and we have since learned that the author of the book was even more anti-Communist than the Foreign Office suspected.

In Nazi Germany, the wrong sort of view - particularly if held by Jews or Army officers opposed to the regime - could lead to an unmarked grave. The German Press saw nothing or heard nothing about any untoward activity. The French were no better during the Algerian campaign. The censor, in the shape of armed troops taking their orders direct from the government, had no compunction about suppressing books, plays or newspapers that even hinted that Arabs were being tortured by the Army. We all know now that they were. Not that the Arabs can claim the moral high ground. Their censors, armed with scissors, simply cut offending articles from foreign newspapers before allowing them to be put on sale. The censor does not, of course, exist in Singapore where self-discipline is one of the island's most admirable traits.

The Communists, Nazis, Fascists and various Asian and African dictators were mainly concerned with the political impact of free speech. They used - and use - censorship to help them cling to power. The Church found it a useful back-up to fire and brimstone. In the age of deference, it was illegal to portray Royalty on the stage, either in theatre or opera. *The Masked Ball*, which deals with the assassination of the King of Sweden, must have caused diplomatic as well as censorial hearts to flutter. In Britain, all stage plays had to be approved by the Lord Chamberlain, a member of the Royal Household. If he didn't like a play, that was it. There was no appeal. It was thanks to the Lord Chamberlain that Pope Pius 12th had a favourable shine put on his wartime inactivity. But eventually his time came and in 1968, after 231 years of preserving 'good manners, decorum and public peace', he was declared redundant. To judge by the vast amount of filth and puerile humour masquerading as comedy that has appeared on the English stage since then, it might not be such a bad idea if he were reinstated.

While the theatre was, to a large extent, concerned with 'entertainment', the embryo film industry lent itself superbly to propaganda. Like the Romans, the powers-that-were recognised the enemy when they saw it and in 1913 set up the British Board of Film Censors. Its task was to ensure that only films 'clean and wholesome and absolutely above suspicion' were passed for exhibition. Within a few years, it ran into trouble with the birth control pioneers, Margaret Sanger and Marie Stopes. Stopes' film, *Maisie's Marriage*, released in 1923, was nothing less than a celluloid version of her best-selling book, *Married Love*. In fact, the film was initially called *Married Love* and sub-titled 'A new contribution to the solution of sexual difficulties'. The book had been published in 1918 and the first birth-control clinics opened in 1921.

118

Incredible though it may seem to cinema-goers in the nineties, when warnings about Aids appear on screens large and small, *Maisie's Marriage* set the BBFC and the Home Office all of a'quiver. The board, headed by the Catholic T.P. O'Connor, found 'many scenes... which render this film unsuitable for exhibition before ordinary audiences... while the title suggests propaganda on a subject unsuitable for discussion in a Cinema Theatre'. The Home Office thought that with a little snip here and there any objectionable material could be easily removed. Samuelson Productions, the makers, apparently agreed to excisions but when the film was shown the BBFC discovered to its horror that the script (it was a silent movie) was intact.

It was at this point that the censor was made to appear quite ridiculous. Despite its avowed intention to keep unsuitable material off the screen, the BBFC actually had no power to prevent a film being shown. Nor had the Home Office. The power was vested in local licensing authorities, such as the London County Council, which decided whether a film was suitable for 'ordinary' people or not. There were some 500 such bodies up and down the country and the vast majority found no threat to morality in Maisie's desire not to have her marriage wrecked by hordes of unwanted children. Such was the hullaballoo that the BBFC - now called the British Board of Film Classification - had to climb down. Today, birth control is the subject of dozens of propaganda films which are regarded as an essential part of health education.

Publishers of books had no censor per se to worry about. They merely had to be careful not to transgress the obscenity laws which covered themes such as lesbianism, adultery and the sexual proclivities of French peasants. If published in Britain, such books might have corrupted the serving wenches of the entire nation. But, of course, that did not stop them being written. James Joyce, struggling to teach English in Trieste, was droning away at *Ulysses* while Lawrence hoped to make a few quid by publishing *Lady Chatterley* in Florence. He did and the book was later brought out in Paris where *Ulysses* first saw the light of day. But what was okay for depraved Continentals was unlikely to get past the moral guardians of HM Customs and Excise and the US Post Office. It was only when the Obscenity Act was replaced by the more liberal Obscene Publications Act in 1959 that publishers felt they could risk bringing out previously banned 'literature'.

What the Obscene Publications Act succeeded in doing, however, was to open the floodgates to pornography. Every kind of four-letter word genius came out of the woodwork to inflict his or her filth on 'ordinary' people. Regrettably, there proved to be no shortage of broad-minded people willing to buy it. Nor was there any shortage of bent coppers willing to turn a blind eye - for the appropriate payment - to material that might still have invited prosecution. For members of Scotland Yard's obscene publications squad, the permissive society meant permission to share the proceeds of pornography. While most of them have been put away or forced to resign, the porn trade continues to thrive. Many of Britain's richest men have made their fortunes by peddling smut.

In the early eighties, sex shops were legalised, prompting Mary Whitehouse to lament 'I never thought I would see the day when a Tory government would license pornography'. Why she thought Tories would be immune to such profitable activities is not entirely clear but matters have certainly not improved. Britain is now a member of the European single market and is virtually powerless to prevent the free movement of goods - including the hard pornography favoured by Dutch, Danes and Swedes - into the United Kingdom. Bookstalls are full of sexually-explicit material while video shops can offer educational tapes featuring bestiality and violent death. On the Internet, one can have unrestricted access to the sick minds of the world. It's hardly surprising that paedophiles, rapists and sexual deviants of all types are inspired to play out their fantasies.

After 30 years of freedom from official control, it's clear

that Roy Jenkins' efforts to make Britain a civilised place have signally failed. Nor has the assertion by Victor Gollancz that 'better an infinity of open drains than a pinpoint of censorship' withstood the test of time. Even Voltaire, the champion of free speech, would have been appalled by what he saw floating in the cesspools of uncensored Britain. He would not, of course, have seen anything by Enid Blyton - a writer far too subversive to let loose on impressionable minds. Nor would he have found any reference to golliwogs among the garbage of a politically-correct but morally-moribund society. As for Sherlock Holmes, Gollancz himself might even have heard rumours that the drug-taking scourge of the underworld was a racist and inclined to call a money-lender a Jew. He would, though, have been able to read *Last Exit to Brooklyn* before throwing up into the open sewer that so appealed to him.

Gollancz, like many liberal publishers, was understandably irked by the obscenity laws that kept authors like Radclyffe Hall and Emile Zola off the list of approved reading. Zola, perhaps, was a bit strong for anybody who had never walked down a country lane and watched the yokels at play. But how anyone, even 70 years ago, could have found *The Well of Loneliness* obscene defies the imagination. Yet, in modern Britain, readers bored with lesbian love can turn to the Internet and learn how to rape an eight-year-old girl.

To the censor, one can only say: Come back, all is forgiven.

Scandal in Belgravia

The fog shrouded Baker Street like a wet blanket, matching my mood as I trudged wearily through the gloom. Even my footsteps were muffled by the fuliginous state of the atmosphere. Only the plaintive whine of a distant busker broke the silence.

I hastened slowly along the pavement, peering at the nondescript doors in my search for Number 423b. Holmes had moved that very morning, evicted from his old lodgings by a building society, and I felt obliged to offer my moral support.

Beyond the grim buildings devoid of architectural merit, I detected a light shining dimly through the fog. It had a luminous quality about it, as though the Devil himself was at work this hour. But at least it wasn't red - a colour from which I had lately been at such pains to wean Holmes.

As I approached, the sound of the busker assumed a more menacing tone. I had encountered the phenomenon once before, on the Bakerloo Line. My hand reached instinctively for my service revolver, nestling unlicensed in my greatcoat pocket.

Suddenly, I realised that the growl came not from a busker but from a huge dog. The luminous glow which I had attributed to the Devil emanated, in fact, from the hound's teeth. These were bared in a distinctly unfriendly fashion.

"Good dog," I said, taking care to avoid the beast, which was tied to the railings outside Number 423b. "I have come to see the master."

At this, the hound positively hurled itself at me, growling savagely as it strained at the leash. Its fangs missed my right leg by two millimetres, or rather less than half an Imperial inch.

A shiver went down my spine as I contemplated the length of frayed rope that secured the beast to the railings. Any minute the rope would snap and I would be at its mercy.

There was only one thing to do. Taking my service revolver, I put a bullet neatly between its jaws. It was a close shot; a very close shot. The sound of the putative busker was stilled

"Sorry about that, old chap," I said. "But your manners were eminently unsuited to an urban environment."

Bounding up the stairs, I deduced from the distinctive smell of marijuana that Holmes was at home.

"Ah, my dear Watson!" he cried as I opened the door and surveyed his new abode. "I have been expecting you."

"I hope I'm not disturbing you," I said as the scourge of the underworld removed a needle from his arm.

"On the contrary," he replied. "You're in the nick of time. I need a new prescription."

I glanced sadly at the pathetic wreck of a man who had once been the world's greatest detective. He looked depressed and washed out. He had never really been the same since his ducking at Reichenbach.

"I hope you don't mind my saying so, Holmes, but you ought to get a grip of yourself. You're becoming an addict."

"Becoming?" said Holmes, hauling himself into a chair by the fire. "What has the present participle to do with it? I became one long ago."

I sat down at the table on which rested the usual pad of blank prescription forms. All I had to do was attach my signature.

"By the way, Holmes, I'm afraid I had to shoot your dog."

"Don't worry, old fellow," said Holmes, sounding almost relieved. "I'm sure the beast had been responsible for a number of curious incidents just lately."

As I examined the mutilated golliwog on a jar of marmalade that unaccountably formed part of the domestic scene, Holmes took a short straw from the mantelpiece and inhaled a quantity of white power. His left nostril twitched uncontrollably before a smile beatified his wizened features.

"How's business?" I asked, wondering how to broach the move from 221 to 423 which, despite the fog, was clearly at the less salubrious end of Baker Street.

"Oh, so so," he muttered. "There is not so much crime

about these days...at least, none that calls for my particular skills of observation and deduction."

"My dear Holmes," I sighed, sorry to see my old friend at such a low ebb, "however did you get into this predicament? I know that your personal habits are not..."

"Cheap?" said Holmes. "No, they're not. And the dog didn't help. I'm glad you have relieved me of that expense."

He paused, sucking his pipe as though trying to summon up courage. I had a feeling that he wanted to tell me something, to unburden his soul. At last, he turned a pair of bloodshot eyes towards me.

"The truth is, Watson, old chap, that I have become emotionally involved with a woman."

"Good lord!" I cried. "Anybody I know?"

"You remember that woman who once got the better of me?"

"Not Irene Adler, the..."

"Jew? The very same."

"Oh, Holmes! How could you?"

"Quite easily," said Holmes, looking a trifle too pleased with himself. "We had been sharing a bottle of claret at one of those low dives off Limehouse...and you know how it is. One thing leads to another."

"And so you are to become a father?"

"I'm afraid so," he confessed.

"Well, at least that should put an end to rumours that you are nothing but a fiddle-playing queer."

"I'm not interested in what those clodhoppers at the Yard think," he said. "They wouldn't know the difference between Jack the Ripper and a Beethoven sonata."

"When is the baby due?" I asked solicitously.

"That is entirely up to you, my dear Watson."

"Up to me? I don't understand."

"You are being even denser than usual," said Holmes, uncharitably. "You're not a Catholic, by any chance?"

"Certainly not."

"Good," said Holmes, poking the fire and sending a great cloud of soot and smoke up the chimney. If the truth be known, he was largely responsible for the filthy state of the air outside. "You see, Watson, I am thinking of opening

124

an abortion clinic."

"An abortion clinic!" I cried, aghast.

"Don't sound so shocked, my dear fellow. Your colleagues in Harley Street have long catered for the miscarriage trade."

"But where will your...customers...come from?"

"Mrs Adler will be the first...and you, my dear Watson, will be her physician."

I was entirely taken aback by this turn of events. Holmes had sunk so low that he was utterly bereft of morality. For a moment, I wished he had broken his neck at the Reichenbach Falls or been attacked by an orang-outang in the mean streets of Paris.

"You see, Watson," he continued. "I must have money. Money by honest means if possible, but, if not, money by any means."

"You have sold your soul to the Devil," I groaned, more sorrowed than angered by this descent into sordid materialism. "Where is your honour, your dignity?"

"Honour?" mused Holmes. "How do you pay the rent with honour? I need money and am prepared to pick up plain brown envelopes, if necessary."

"I thought you were going to open an abortion clinic?"

"And how do you think the elegant young ladies who frequent it are going to pay?" he asked sarcastically. "By asking their husbands to write out a cheque?"

"Really, Holmes! I've never heard of anything so unethical in all my life."

"Then you must have led a very sheltered life. If you had suffered from cold turkey, as I have, on every day of the year, except Christmas, and been turned out with only the bare necessities of life, you would not be so smug."

He filled his pipe nonchalently from the pot market 'pot' by the fireside.

"But I intend to wrench you out of your complacency," he said. "I have decided to appoint you as chief obstretician."

"By God, Holmes, I'll not do it!" I cried, staring at my erstwhile friend with indignation, tinged with disgust.

"There is little point in invoking God," replied Holmes unctuously. "Mammon might be more appropriate."

"There is no God but God!" I exclaimed. "I am a follower of the Prophet Mohamed."

"Ah" muttered Holmes, raising his eyebrows slightly. "A closet Mussulman. I knew you were hiding something from me."

"I am hiding nothing," I declared, my cheeks reddening. "Even if you have abandoned yourself to the Devil, I at least retain some shred of moral fibre."

"And long may it keep you in beer and baccy," said Holmes, glancing at the hookah in the corner of the room. "I wish I could afford the luxury of your beliefs."

He studied his fingernails for a few moments and then said quietly: "So, my dear Watson, you are a Moslem. Am I to conclude, therefore, that you hate the Jews?"

I saw what he was getting at. Irene Adler, the cause of his distress, was one of the chosen people.

"I had always thought you were not terribly fond of them yourself," I remarked bitterly.

"Times change," replied Holmes with a shrug. "You don't think I could impregnate a person whom I found abhorent?"

"You are quite capable of anything when you are up to your neck in dope and claret," I said, striding towards the door. "It's all over between us, Holmes. You are beyond redemption."

"Not so fast," said Holmes, blowing out a cloud of marijuana smoke. "How will you explain that unlicensed pistol should I be inclined to raise the matter with my friends at the Yard?"

"So, you stoop even to blackmail?" I retorted contemptuously. "You really are a pathetic creature, Holmes. May God help you when you become a father."

He moved to detain me by putting a foot in the door.

"Out of my way!" I cried. "I'm off to the mosque for evening prayers. Remember, there is no God but God."

"On the contrary," said Holmes, "there is no god but money."

I slammed the door and hurried down the stairs. The

126

dog was still on the pavement, its blood running down the gutter. The fog was as thick as ever.

I leaned against the street lamp to catch my breath. I wondered what would become of the once-great detective, now wallowing in the cesspit that was the heart of the Empire. His pathological desire for money, coupled with sexual incontinence, had destroyed years of friendship.

My heart was beating so fast that I barely heard the approach of a cab. I was about to hail it when it stopped and a bearded figure got out. Stepping over the dead dog, he let himself swiftly into Number 423b and disappeared from view.

I turned my attention to the carriage. It was not, as I had first thought, a public conveyance but a private brougham. There was a coat of arms on the side that I could not make out in the gloom. The driver sat motionless, staring straight ahead with an air of professional disinterestedness.

My thoughts returned to the passenger. What was a person of such distinguished, even regal, bearing doing in such a locality on such a murky day? Could it be, I wondered, that Holmes was already soliciting clients for his clinic among the aristocracy?

Suddenly, all became clear. I knew where I had seen the bearded figure before. It was at a house in London where I had gone to treat a Colonel Keppel. Surely...

On the verge of despair, I made my way briskly towards the mosque.

15

The backlash

A lot of people have clearly done quite well out of political correctness. To judge by the level of cant that pollutes the airwaves, it has been the growth industry of the decade. Lawyers, lobbyists and liberated loopies have all battled to win the hearts and minds of a gullible public - as well as a share of the money at stake. PR men teach their clients how to win contracts and avoid Ratnerisms. Publishers looking for the next bestseller print the views of loony Left and raving Right. Patients, citizens and British Rail customers all have their own charter, even if they have to wait two hours for a train or sleep on the floor because the NHS is short of funds. Everywhere, the true meaning of words is distorted to protect an over-sensitive minority. No matter that the intellectual premise is false; just emit a steady stream of drivel and you will be politically correct.

In the United States, almost any piece of legislation - civil or criminal - can be given a p.c. slant. Punks with purple hair, or no hair at all in the pubic region, can file suit alleging discrimination, even posthumously if he/she couldn't read and smoked 60 cigarettes a day. Rapes, lynchings and the inevitable lootings all have to be colour-corrected before being shown on television. In London, seven-figure salaries are sold to the workforce in terms that ought to make shareholders weep - but don't. New, improved varieties of soap powder that won't choke baby seals or rot men's underpants are promoted with a p.c. label. Who but a cynic would think that concern for the environment was simply part of the marketing strategy?

As for the little woman (the fragrant bit of tail, not the statutory whore of the boardroom), she can make life difficult for predatory males by alleging sexual harassment of the incorrect kind. In fact, a lot of women quite enjoy being sexually harassed; it makes them feel feminine and worth all the effort of painting their toe-nails. Only the sour old haridans whose bottoms have never been pinched regard such activities as sexploitation.

There have inevitably been casualties on the road to political correctness. The Royal Family, the head of which now pays income tax like the rest of us, has been among the losers. Petulent princesses (alas, no longer with us) and debt-ridden duchesses with scant regard for the monarchy have undermined the proprieties of palace life. A measure of farce and vulgarity has crept in. Protocol is not what it was. Deference is on the way out - unless, of course, a semi-detached member of the family kills herself after a night on the spree in Paris. And if the Prime Minister of Australia puts a republican arm around the Queen of England who will object if the lady herself doesn't? Only the jealous matrons of Melbourne suburbs, if not the megastar of Moonee Ponds, might think the P.M. was being p.i.

The unions, too, have seen their influence wane under the impact of corrective legislation. Politically-motivated labour laws, designed to keep wages down, have encouraged many brothers to jump ship and look after Number One. Collective bargaining, along with picket lines and expressions of solidarity, are out. Strikes are as rare as sightings of the Great Bustard at Wapping. The unions have been taught not to get above their stations. Not that they will fare any better under New Labour. To remind the party that union funds help it to fight elections is not only politically incorrect but an affront to the middle-class values espoused by the New Leader. To sing the Red Flag at the party's annual conference is tantamount to insurrection. The Red Flag is a reminder of the party's socialist past - and socialism is not what New Labour is about.

The fashionable way to support Labour these days is to wear a suit and pretend to be a Tory. The politically-correct socialite does not eat mushy peas or mention the Co-op although it is perfectly acceptable to send one's children to a private or grant-maintained school. Strangely enough, it is the unions - so often branded as dinosaurs - that are leading the way back to reality. They are not above saying that greed and self-interest are the same old Tory values, whichever party adopts them and whatever fancy names they are given.

One of the words to appear with ever-increasing frequency in the Tory litany of economic hocus-pocus is 'competition'. Like Guinness, competition is supposed to be good for you, especially if you are a shareholder in a company that has managed to break the power of the unions. That untrammelled competition leads to a sweatshop economy in which workers are forced to undercut one another is cynically brushed aside. Indeed, the idea that workers should compete for their daily bread while shareholders sit back and reap the rewards has become part of the conventional wisdom. The only mystery is why the unions have allowed such an endearing legacy of Thatcherism to survive. Nobody, it seems, has ever read John Steinbeck's novel of the depressed thirties, *The Grapes of Wrath*. Steinbeck showed exactly what happens when competition is allowed free rein. The weak go to the wall and the benefits go entirely to the employer. (These are the very same employers who are so opposed to a statutory minimum wage.) Of all the weasel words spawned by the architects of political correctness, competition - or the law of the jungle - is the most invidious. There is nothing intrinsically good about competition; in fact, it can be positively harmful, as many thousands of ex-workers in the gas, water and electricity industries will confirm. The only beneficiaries of the new 'competitive environment' in these natural monopolies have been the shareholders and the fat cats in the boardroom. Everybody else has had to pay through the nose.

Like all growth industries, political correctness is a child of fashion - and, like all fashions, eventually becomes dated. Who now wears flowers in their hair or pickets nuclear missile sites? To have been a member of CND in the sixties and seventies, when dissent was in the air, was the fashionable way to protest against the futility of war. Viewed from the nineties, when the Berlin Wall is no more, the movement has an aura of faded gentility about it. The debate and the protesters have moved on. Many have taken jobs, mortgaging their future to the European Union instead of writing it off under the threat of nuclear annihilation. The Britain of Cedric Brown, with its peace dividends and non-dissenting shareholders, is a very different place to that of the lean and hungry pussies of Greenham Common.

Just as the Cultural Revolution proved to be the high point of political correctness in China, the excesses of loonyism have ensured its decline in the West. In California, white, Anglo-Saxon protestants, sick to death of seeing their jobs go to blacks, Hispanics and illegal immigrants, have launched a counter attack. They are demanding an end to the positive discrimination which favours 'under-privileged and under-represented' members of the society. Positive discrimination is now seen for what it is: discrimination. Not surprisingly, the ethnic minorities which have enjoyed their new status at the head of the jobs queue are not too keen for equal opportunities to be restored. They regard any swing of the pendulum as an infringement of their 'rights'. The pendulum is nevertheless gaining momentum.

As a fashionable way to appear loony without really trying, political correctness has had its day. There will, of course, always be new fashions to bend the mind and seduce the impressionable. The Right-wing thugs who follow Monsieur le Pen in France are a constant reminder that the void is waiting to be filled. But most men and women are tired of addressing one another as chairs and pretending that sexual differences don't exist. They want to get back to saying what they mean, in language that everyone can understand. There are already enough laws on the statute book to prevent the stirring up of racial hatred, the bashing of queers and the abuse of children. For every one-legged black lesbian who deserves our support there are dozens of multi-ethnic drug dealers who ought to be put down. For every liberal Home Secretary with a taste for literature there are scores of dirty old men with a penchant for paedophilia. For every special constable there is a peeping tom with an ulterior motive. For every Dennis Skinner there is a small army of mealy-mouthed politicians only too ready to embrace the next fashion if it will help to keep their seats.

The question is: what will the next fashion look like? Will it reflect the views of neo-Nazis in Germany or the surfies of Bondi beach? Will the loonier notions of the trendy Lefties, which are largely responsible for the current backlash, somehow retain their grip on the national psyche? And what of the Up-U culture, in which amoral little boys and girls will sell their grandmother down the river, so long as it is profitable? To ensure that political correctness is not replaced by something far uglier, we must begin by removing the layers of false morality that have been applied over the years. Only then will the problems of society be seen in their true light.

If political correctness has taught us anything, it is that you don't get rid of a problem by calling it something else.

Late final extra!

Are you now, or have you ever been, a droopy groupie? Don't be ashamed or afraid to answer. You are in good company. In the thirties, millions of groupies outside the Soviet Union thought that droopies - as worn by Uncle Joe - were the best thing since unsliced rye bread. To stoop in groups at the temple of Dzhugashvily was a favourite pastime of the British intelligentsia who often went to Russia specifically for that purpose. Those who knew better went to Mexico where they drooped under the sudden impact of an ice pick.

Or perhaps you are a groovy loopy, hoping to adopt a poor, undernourished child that otherwise would be laid to rest on a Chinese hillside? Most loopies are themselves only children at heart and not averse to a little raving if they don't get their way. To some people, they appear quite loony. The real loonies (in a p.c. context) are completely round the twist and tend to avoid groups as they are, in fact, loners. This makes it essential for the Neighbourhood Watch to raise the alarm the moment one is spotted entering a restricted zone with an unlicensed newt.

Moonies - who include loonies, loopies and droopy groupies - seldom gather in groups of less than four thousand, ostensibly to get married but, in fact, to engage in a groovy group grope. This can be even more upsetting than a Rolling Newt concert on the village green. In some cases, a really groovy group grope with musical accompaniment will reduce the creepie peepies of the Neighbourhood Watch to tears, making the boys in blue think they are dealing with a bunch of weepie peepies. This can have serious implications for the drive to recruit special constables.

How, then, does one disavow the past and embark on a career of political incorrectness? One possibility is to enrol at an ashram where a swami or guru will show you The

Way. In the sixties, many of the world's most beautiful people could be found in the Himalayas, eating lentils and looking for God. Unfortunately, most of the gurus were in California, looking for dollars. As Kipling had predicted, the twain were destined ne'er to meet.

The recent downturn in the economy has meant, however, that the supply of gurus once again exceeds demand. This makes it fairly easy to find one. For many Britons, the search could begin and end at the Jobcentre. All they need is a bicycle and they will see the light. (It won't be turned on for them, however. Some things they must do for themselves.)

The regime is strict. No backsliding, no flowers in the hair, rings through the nose or praying to Lotto. All business suits to be returned to Oxfam by six o'clock. It's not surprising that after a hard day in the saddle many searchers begin to droop and think that the moustachio'd Georgian was not such a bad chap, after all. He might have been loony (and possibly incorrect) but, then, so are a lot of people - and not all of them eat lentils or keep newts in the bath.

What to do if you have been offended by this book.

1. Take it back to the bookseller and demand a refund. Booksellers are usually very helpful in this respect and will make only a taken deduction for dog-eared or torn pages, coffee stains, etc.

2. Exert your rights under the Citizen's Charter. As these are difficult to define, you will have ample scope to make up whatever silly story you like.

3. Complain to the Race Relations Board and/or the Chief Rabbi. The former will take the publisher to court and, using taxpayers' money, sue him for being beastly to black men. The Chief Rabbi will probably declare a fatwa - provided the Arabs can spare one.

4. Ring your MP, preferably in the middle of the night, and complain that there is a red under your bed. If your MP is ex-directory or has McCarthyite tendencies of his own, try the Neighbourhood Watch. As a last resort, wait in a loopy loo until the light dawns.

5. Take a long, hard look at yourself in the mirror. If no sign of hypocrisy is present, get yourself analysed without delay. You have lost your sense of humour and are in a bad way. Avoid bookshops in future.

About the author

Keith Sharp is the author of four previous books, all on a financial theme. He was born near Orpington, Kent, in 1938 and has lived in Australia, New Zealand, Canada and North Africa. During National Service, he spent two years with Army Public Relations in Singapore and Hong Kong. He was a television reporter for Channel 9, Brisbane, and as a freelance journalist has written for all the non-tabloid Fleet Street dailies. His sixth book, Aunt Edna's Guide to Paradise, is due out shortly. Like How to be Politically Incorrect, it will be published by Haberfield Editions, the author's own imprint.